The Mission is Critical: Mastering Hyperscale Data Centers

Justin DeFillippo

Published by Justin DeFillippo, 2024.

THE MISSION IS CRITICAL: MASTERING HYPERSCALE DATA CENTERS

First edition. September 13, 2024.

ISBN: 979-8227315151

Written by Justin DeFillippo.

Table of Contents

To: My Daughters & Family

Milana & Vienna,

May your dreams be as big as a hyperscale data center.

And to my family: I did it—I wrote the book on it!

I love you all.

The Mission is Critical: Mastering Hyperscale Data Centers
"A Guide by Justin DeFillippo—From the Man Who Literally Wrote the Book on Building Hyperscale Data Centers."

Justin DeFillippo

About the Author:

Justin DeFillippo is a multifaceted professional whose career spans over 25 years in the mission-critical construction and data center industry. He started his journey as an electrician in the heart of New York City, known for being the fastest and most unforgiving construction market in the world. Surviving in such a relentless environment meant adapting quickly, working harder than the next person, and constantly proving oneself—values that Justin embodies to this day.

From a young age, Justin developed a love for animals, a passion he shares with his wife, Sandra. Together, they dream of starting an animal sanctuary where all animals, regardless of their background, can find a safe and loving home. Their rescue dog, Butkus, a Black Mouth Cur from Harlem, NYC, is a testament to their commitment to this dream and serves as a constant reminder of the joy and unconditional love that animals bring into their lives.

Justin is also a dedicated family man who takes immense pride in his role as a father. Everything he does is driven by the love for his children and his desire to create a better future for them. His roots in Brooklyn have instilled in him the spirit of an underdog always ready for a prize fight, never backing down from a challenge, and always striving for excellence.

Throughout his career, Justin has made it a personal mission to empower others in the trades, teaching them that they are more than just a number on a spreadsheet. He believes in the importance of mentorship, and he takes pride in helping those he meets along the way, ensuring they know their value and potential in an industry that often overlooks the individual.

Justin's journey wasn't straightforward—he attended law school at St. John's University through the ARMY ROTC program, which shaped his discipline and strategic thinking. With a vast array of certifications, including those in photovoltaic systems and EPA Universal Certification for refrigerants, Justin has demonstrated a relentless commitment to mastering every aspect of his trade.

He's spent years honing his craft, not just through the hands-on work of an electrician but by mastering the business end of contracting like a champion. As a 'fixer' and problem solver, Justin has built a reputation for being the go-to guy who can navigate complex projects and lead them to success.

Justin dreams big, whether it's his quest for a 1989 Ferrari Mondial T or his vision of a simplified approach to construction and data center projects. He believes in getting back to basics, cutting through unnecessary complexities, and focusing on the core elements—size, capacity, power, redundancy, uptime, and cost. To him, the success of any project is about making smart decisions, planning well, and always keeping it simple.

Justin's goal is to help others find the same success by sharing his no-nonsense, real-world insights. Through this book, he hopes to guide those in the industry to streamline their projects, reduce stress, and always aim for quality in every aspect of their work. For Justin, it's all about the journey and the people you meet along the way, and he wishes nothing but the best for everyone he encounters.

What This Book Is About and Who It's For

The Mission is Critical: Mastering Hyperscale Data Centers is for everyone in the hyperscale data center space—whether you're already in the industry, curious about it, or looking to break into the sector. This book offers an in-depth exploration of the complexities involved in designing, constructing, and operating these critical facilities. Well, I sure hope it does... If not I'm sure you can find a YouTube video on it...

Scope of the Book (SOB)

The primary goal of this book is to serve as a practical guide for anyone involved in the hyperscale data center industry. Whether you're stepping into this space for the first time or you're a seasoned professional aiming to stay ahead of the curve, this book has you covered. It addresses nearly every aspect of the data center lifecycle, from initial site selection, design, and construction to commissioning and ongoing operations. Along the way, you'll find personal insights into the latest tech advancements (I will try not to date the information as the industry is growing so fast), best practices, and lessons learned from real-world case studies. Importantly, I'll also highlight what not to do—there's no sugarcoating here. While I'll try to avoid specifics that could quickly become outdated, the focus will be on principles that stand the test of time.

So, Justin...Who Is This Book For?

Here's the deal: For some reason, this sector often seems closed off, shrouded in secrecy as if everything about it is top-secret. Like we're all spies living in a movie and driving an Aston Martin down to Monte Carlo... While confidentiality is crucial when it comes to clients—and that's something we all respect—the notion that this space is somehow "specialized" or "hush hush" beyond all comprehension is nonsense. RUBBISH I TELL YA! People, might pitch it as if it's rocket science, but here's the truth: It's just construction. That's it! No big deal! Sure, there are specific things you need to know and I will talk about all of it. At the end of the day, if you can read specs, you can handle data centers just like any other project.

Who else is this book for Justin?

Industry Professionals

If you're an engineer, architect, project manager, general contractor, subcontractor, third-party manager, or consultant working in the data center industry, this book will provide you with the technical knowledge and practical insights needed to excel. It's not going to teach you how to be a PM or an architect—that's your job—but it will offer considerations and ideas that might not have crossed your mind. This book covers the nuts and bolts of data center design and construction, giving you the tools to sharpen your expertise.

Business Executives and Decision Makers

If you're an executive, decision-maker, or part of an investment group in technology, finance, e-commerce, or any sector eyeing the future, this book provides a strategic perspective on data center development. It will help you understand the critical decisions involved in building and operating a data center—from choosing the right location and securing power to managing costs and ensuring uptime. Most importantly, it will show you how to avoid getting upsold on proprietary tech or other costly traps. Let's be blunt—I don't want anyone taking advantage of you.

Students and Academics

For students and academics studying data center technology, computer science, or related fields, this book serves as a comprehensive reference. It bridges the gap between theory and practice, offering insights you won't find in a classroom. Whether you're working on a paper, preparing for a career, or just expanding your knowledge, this book is a valuable resource. Remember that more than half the books out there are written from someone who never swung a hammer...

Curious Minds

Maybe you picked this up for a plane ride, or perhaps your grandma bought it for you because you built her a computer once (we all have that one family member, right?). Whatever the reason, if you're curious about this space, I hope you'll find something valuable in these pages. The principles discussed here extend beyond just data centers—they're applicable across the entire construction industry and life...

In short, this book is for anyone who wants to understand hyperscale data centers, whether you're in the industry, considering joining it, or simply curious.

Topics We Will Discuss

Well, the meat and potatoes aka content will be divided into a whole bunch of sections, each focusing on a different aspects of data center development and operation. Here's a brief rundown of what you can expect:

1. **Introduction: Defining the Purpose of a Hyperscale Data Center** We begin by exploring the various purposes hyperscale data centers serve, from supporting AI and cloud computing to enabling financial transactions and e-commerce. Understanding the purpose of the data center is crucial, as it guides every decision in the design and construction process.
2. **Location Considerations: Choosing the Right Site** Next, we delve into the critical factors influencing site selection, including proximity to fiber infrastructure, utility availability, geographical factors, and the regulatory environment. We also discuss the importance of edge networks in reducing latency, particularly in

sectors like finance where milliseconds matter.

3. **Site Acquisition and Environmental Impact** This section covers the process of acquiring land for a data center, whether by purchasing existing buildings or developing new sites. It emphasizes the importance of conducting thorough environmental impact assessments and engaging with the local community to address concerns about jobs, traffic, and aesthetics.
4. **Design and Engineering: Laying the Foundation** We then focus on the design and engineering aspects of data center construction, from creating baseline plans to integrating sustainability features. Key engineering requirements such as electrical infrastructure, cooling systems, and network infrastructure are covered, along with the importance of security and compliance.
5. **Vendor Selection and Management** Selecting and managing vendors is a critical part of any data center project. This section provides guidance on identifying key vendors, negotiating contracts, and ensuring vendors are bondable and insured. It also discusses the importance of maintaining strong vendor relationships and the role of procurement strategy in ensuring timely material delivery.

1. **Construction and Project Management** Here, we delve into the construction phase, emphasizing the importance of pre-construction planning, phased construction approaches, and rigorous project management. Best

practices for managing health and safety on the construction site, including the use of third-party vendors to ensure neutrality, are also covered.

2. **Commissioning and Testing** Before a data center can go live, it must undergo a thorough commissioning and testing process. This section outlines the different levels of commissioning, from factory acceptance testing to integrated systems testing, and provides guidance on navigating AHJ inspections and obtaining final certifications.
3. **Data Center Operations** Once the data center is operational, effective management is key to maintaining uptime and efficiency. We cover establishing standard operating procedures (SOPs), maintenance schedules, and monitoring systems. The importance of vendor management and security, including the need for MSAs and third-party vetting, is also discussed.
4. **Case Studies: Lessons from the Field** Real-world examples of successful hyperscale data centers across various sectors are presented here, highlighting the lessons learned and best practices that emerged from these projects. The case studies emphasize the importance of documentation, flexibility, and continuous improvement.
5. **The business end/The end:** We explores strategic business models for hyperscale data centers, emphasizing passive income through infrastructure leasing, minimal technology investment, and cautious market expansion to maximize profitability and reduce risk.

1. **Justin's CO** (Closeout)

I want to just give you a bit more advice and I saved it for the last chapter. Juicy!

SO, IN ESSENCE:

The Mission is Critical is more than just a technical manual—it's a strategic guide for navigating the complexities of the data center industry. Whether you're building a new facility, managing an existing one, or simply looking to understand the forces shaping the future of digital infrastructure, this book provides the insights and knowledge you need to succeed, offering a deeper understanding of the mission-critical sector.

Before we move forward, let's define what exactly a Hyperscale Data Center is—as simply as possible. Justin's note: house vs. mansion: What's the difference? One is much bigger and has everything the house has only its bigger and better...

A hyperscale data center is a massive facility designed to support the needs of large-scale internet companies and cloud service providers. Think of it like this: it's just a huge building filled with a lot of computers. Nothing more, nothing less. Typically, these data centers serve a single client. Once multiple clients are housed in the data center, it becomes a large colocation (colo) data center, where anyone can rent space. However, ask yourself—what sounds better: colo or hyperscale? Which has more money to spend, borrow, or invest? If you answered hyperscale, you're right!

In layman's terms, a hyperscale data center is like a really, really big engine room that keeps the internet running. That's it.

Chapter 1: The "What" is the Data Center Going to Do and Why Defining It Is Vital

WHEN EMBARKING ON THE journey of building a hyperscale data center, one of the most critical steps is defining its purpose—essentially, determining what the data center is going to do and why. Hyperscale data centers are massive facilities designed to support large-scale operations, from AI and cloud computing to Bitcoin mining and beyond. Defining the purpose of the data center isn't just a high-level goal; it's the foundation upon which every subsequent decision is built. Whether the data center will be used for AI, cloud storage, Bitcoin mining, or any other application, defining its purpose early on is crucial. This definition will dictate its design, infrastructure, location, and operational strategies, ensuring that the data center is optimized for its intended function and can save both time and resources down the line.

If you're thinking, "If we build it, they will come," you need to know that such an approach won't work in the hyperscale data center space. A clear, defined purpose from the start is essential. In this chapter, we'll explore the various potential uses for a data center, classifying them by their power demands, latency requirements, and other critical factors that will influence their design and location. Forgive me if I sound "redundant" but... I need to drive certain points home. We will also delve into additional considerations that are essential for ensuring the long-term success of the project/business.

Defining the Purpose: The Cornerstone of Success

UNDERSTANDING AND DEFINING the purpose of a data center is not just important—it is absolutely essential. This defined purpose will shape every aspect of the project, from the ground up. Let's take a closer look at why defining the purpose is crucial:

1. Impact on Design

THE PURPOSE OF THE data center directly influences its architectural design, including the physical layout, cooling systems, and power distribution. For example:

- **AI and High-Performance Computing (HPC):** A data center designed for AI or HPC might require specialized rooms for high-density cabinets or racks, along with advanced cooling systems to manage the significant heat generated by densely packed GPUs and other specialized hardware.
- **Cloud Storage:** A data center focused on cloud storage might prioritize scalable storage solutions and efficient power distribution to handle large amounts of data with flexibility. This could involve designing modular spaces that can easily expand as storage needs grow.

The design also impacts the facility's future-proofing. For example, a data center supporting AI might need to accommodate rapid technological advancements, requiring a design that allows for easy upgrades or expansions. Justin's notes: Okay with that being said. You need to stay away from proprietary power systems that will end up costing you in time and money to make the simplest changes. Don't worry we'll talk about this later.

2. Infrastructure Requirements

THE SPECIFIC USE CASE will determine the infrastructure needs of the data center:

- **Power-Intensive Applications:** Industries like Bitcoin mining require robust power supplies and may benefit from being located near inexpensive energy sources. These data centers might also need advanced cooling systems to manage the significant heat generated by the mining process.
- **Latency-Sensitive Applications:** For industries like high-frequency trading, ultra-fast networking infrastructure is essential to ensure minimal latency. This need for speed will influence everything from the data center's geographical location to the type of networking hardware used.

The infrastructure also includes backup power solutions, cooling technologies, and security systems tailored to the data center's specific needs. For instance, data centers that handle sensitive information may require additional layers of physical and cyber security.

3. Location Selection

THE GEOGRAPHICAL LOCATION of the data center is heavily influenced by its intended purpose:

- **Latency-Sensitive Applications:** Financial services and gaming applications require proximity to end-users or financial hubs to minimize latency. This means choosing a location close to these centers is crucial for success.
- **Power-Intensive Operations:** Operations like cryptocurrency mining benefit from being near low-cost

energy sources, even if these locations are remote. The availability of renewable energy sources, such as hydroelectric power, can also be a significant factor in location selection.

Other location considerations include climate, which can impact cooling requirements, and local regulations, which may influence construction and operational permits. Additionally, accessibility to skilled labor and proximity to critical infrastructure, like fiber optic networks, are also vital considerations.

4. Scalability Considerations

THE DEFINED PURPOSE also influences the scalability of the data center:

- **Future-Proofing:** As technology evolves, the data center must be able to scale in response to growing data needs, expanding user bases, or evolving technologies. For example, a data center supporting AI might need to scale rapidly as AI applications become more widespread, requiring modular designs that allow for easy expansion.
- **Operational Flexibility:** The ability to adapt to changing market demands is crucial. For instance, a data center initially designed for cloud storage might later need to accommodate AI workloads, requiring a flexible infrastructure that can handle diverse demands.

Scalability also involves planning for potential increases in power and cooling requirements, ensuring that the data center can grow without significant disruptions to operations.

5. Regulatory and Compliance Factors

DIFFERENT DATA CENTER purposes come with varying regulatory and compliance requirements:

- **Financial Services:** Data centers serving financial institutions must comply with stringent regulations like PCI DSS, which governs how financial data is stored and processed. This will influence everything from the security systems implemented to the reporting protocols followed.
- **Healthcare Data:** Data centers handling healthcare information must comply with regulations such as HIPAA, which mandates strict security and privacy measures.

Compliance also extends to environmental regulations, particularly for data centers with significant energy consumption or waste output. Ensuring adherence to these regulations is critical for avoiding legal complications and maintaining operational integrity.

6. Sustainability and Environmental Impact

SUSTAINABILITY IS INCREASINGLY becoming a critical factor in data center design:

- **Energy-Intensive Applications:** For applications like AI or Bitcoin mining, the environmental impact can be significant. Implementing renewable energy solutions or advanced cooling techniques can help mitigate this impact and align the data center with broader sustainability goals.
- **Environmental Regulations:** Depending on the location and the type of operations, the data center might need to comply with local environmental regulations, which can affect everything from energy sourcing to waste management.

Sustainability also includes considerations for water usage, especially in regions where water is scarce. Data centers can implement advanced cooling technologies that reduce water consumption or explore alternative methods like air cooling.

7. Risk Management

UNDERSTANDING THE PURPOSE of the data center is essential for effective risk management:

- **Operational Risks:** Different applications come with different levels of operational risk. For instance, data centers supporting disaster recovery must prioritize redundancy and resilience to ensure continuous operation in case of an emergency.
- **Cybersecurity Risks:** For data centers handling sensitive information, such as financial data or government

operations, cybersecurity must be a top priority. This requires robust security protocols and regular audits to prevent breaches.

Risk management also includes planning for natural disasters, power outages, and other unforeseen events. Data centers must have contingency plans in place to ensure minimal disruption to services.

8. Technology Roadmap Alignment

THE PURPOSE OF THE data center should align with a long-term technology roadmap:

- **Staying Relevant:** As technology evolves, the data center must adapt to remain competitive. This means planning for future upgrades, such as transitioning to newer, more efficient cooling systems or integrating AI-driven automation for operations.
- **Innovative Integration:** Data centers must be prepared to integrate emerging technologies that can enhance efficiency, reduce costs, or improve performance. This includes exploring the potential of AI, machine learning, and other cutting-edge solutions.

Aligning the data center with a technology roadmap ensures that it remains a valuable asset in the long term, capable of adapting to new challenges and opportunities.

9. Stakeholder Involvement

EARLY INVOLVEMENT OF all relevant stakeholders is crucial:

- **Collaborative Planning:** Clients, investors, IT teams (if need be), and local governments should be involved early in the planning process to ensure that the data center's purpose aligns with business goals, regulatory requirements, and community expectations.
- **Transparency:** Open communication with stakeholders helps build trust and ensures that all parties are aligned on the project's objectives and challenges.

Involving stakeholders from the beginning can also help identify potential issues before they become critical, ensuring smoother project execution.

Industry-Specific Use Cases: Tailoring the Data Center to Its Purpose

NOW THAT WE'VE DISCUSSED why defining the purpose is so crucial, let's look at some specific industry use cases to understand how these factors come into play:

AI, Machine Learning, and High-Performance Computing (HPC)

- **Power Draw:** Very High
- **Latency Importance:** Very High
- **Location Considerations:** Proximity to urban centers and research hubs

- **Key Notes:** Workloads for AI and HPC require significant computing power and low latency to process and analyze large data sets efficiently. Hyperscale data centers dedicated to this industry must support high-performance computing (HPC) with advanced cooling systems to manage the heat generated by densely packed GPUs and TPUs.

Cloud Storage and Computing

- **Power Draw:** Moderate
- **Latency Importance:** Low to Moderate
- **Location Considerations:** Flexibility in location, often near major hubs
- **Key Notes:** Cloud computing and storage data centers provide the backbone for delivering services over the internet. These centers need low latency to ensure responsive service delivery. Their location is often chosen based on proximity to major internet exchanges and business hubs to reduce latency and improve user experience.

Bitcoin and Cryptocurrency Mining

- **Power Draw:** Very High
- **Latency Importance:** Low
- **Location Considerations:** Proximity to cheap, abundant power, preferably in colder climates
- **Key Notes:** Cryptocurrency mining is one of the most power-intensive uses for a data center. These centers are

often located near inexpensive and abundant power sources, such as hydroelectric plants. Latency is less of a concern, allowing these centers to be situated in more remote areas.

Justin's notes: Great business, low cost of entry into the data center world.

Financial Services and High-Frequency Trading (HFT)

- **Power Draw:** Moderate
- **Latency Importance:** Extremely High
- **Location Considerations:** Close proximity to financial hubs and stock exchanges
- **Key Notes:** For financial services and HFT, speed is the most critical factor. Data centers serving this industry must be located as close as possible to financial hubs to minimize latency, which can significantly impact trading outcomes.

E-Commerce Platforms

- **Power Draw:** Moderate to High
- **Latency Importance:** High
- **Location Considerations:** Near major urban centers and logistics hubs
- **Key Notes:** E-commerce data centers support online transactions, inventory management, and customer databases. Low latency is crucial for a smooth shopping

experience, particularly during high-traffic periods like Black Friday.

Social Media Platforms

- **Power Draw:** Moderate to High
- **Latency Importance:** High
- **Location Considerations:** Near large user populations
- **Key Notes:** Social media platforms generate and process vast amounts of data, requiring data centers that can handle high bandwidth traffic and deliver content with low latency. These centers are typically located near large user populations.

Video Streaming Services

- **Power Draw:** High
- **Latency Importance:** High
- **Location Considerations:** Near content delivery points and major population centers
- **Key Notes:** Video streaming services require data centers that can deliver large volumes of data quickly and without interruption. Latency is critical, so these centers are often situated near content delivery points.

Disaster Recovery and Business Continuity

- **Power Draw:** Variable
- **Latency Importance:** Low to Moderate
- **Location Considerations:** Geographically diverse, away

from primary data centers

- **Key Notes:** Disaster recovery data centers provide backup solutions in case of an emergency. These centers are strategically located to eliminate the risk of a single disaster impacting both primary and backup sites.

Government and Defense

- **Power Draw:** Moderate to High
- **Latency Importance:** High for certain applications
- **Location Considerations:** Secure, often near government facilities
- **Key Notes:** Data centers handling sensitive government and defense information require high levels of security and redundancy. Latency is critical for certain applications, such as real-time data analysis.

Telecommunications

- **Power Draw:** Somewhat High
- **Latency Importance:** High
- **Location Considerations:** Near communication hubs and major cities
- **Key Notes:** Telecommunications data centers support voice, data, and video communication services. Latency is a significant factor, particularly for services like VoIP or video conferencing.

Space Exploration and Satellite Operations

- **Power Draw:** High
- **Latency Importance:** High for satellite operations, moderate for space exploration
- **Location Considerations:** Near space agencies, ground stations, or research institutions
- **Key Notes:** Data centers supporting space exploration handle vast amounts of data from satellites and other extraterrestrial missions. These operations need low latency, particularly for managing communications with orbiting satellites.

Colocation (COLO) Data Centers

- **Power Draw:** Variable, depending on tenant needs
- **Latency Importance:** High
- **Location Considerations:** Near business hubs, tech centers, and major urban areas
- **Key Notes:** Colocation data centers provide space, power, cooling, and physical security for multiple customers' servers and networking equipment. These data centers are strategically located near business hubs to reduce latency for tenants.

See why defining the mission is important right?

DEFINING THE MISSION of a hyperscale data center is the cornerstone of its development. Whether the data center is intended for AI, cloud storage, Bitcoin mining, financial services, or any other application, the specific use case will guide every decision, from the design and infrastructure requirements to location and operations. This targeted approach ensures that the data center is built to perform optimally for its intended function, providing the foundation for success in a fast-paced and ever-evolving digital landscape.

By understanding the specific needs and challenges associated with each use case, you can make informed decisions that will drive the success of your data center project. The defined purpose will ensure that resources are allocated efficiently, risks are managed effectively, and the facility is capable of scaling to meet future demands. Ultimately, a well-defined purpose is what will set your hyperscale data center apart in an increasingly competitive and technologically advanced industry.

Get it got it good let's take a look back before we go forward:

WITH THE MISSION CLEARLY defined, the next step is to consider how to choose the ideal location for your data center—a decision that will have lasting implications for both performance and cost. In the next chapter, we'll get into the factors that make or break a data center site, exploring everything from proximity to fiber infrastructure to the availability of renewable energy sources.

Chapter 2: Location Considerations: Choosing the Right Site

SELECTING THE RIGHT location for a hyperscale data center is not just a geographical decision; it is a strategic choice that has long-lasting implications on performance, costs, scalability, and future growth. The site you choose will directly impact your data center's ability to meet latency requirements, ensure energy efficiency, comply with regulations, and withstand natural and man-made disasters. A poor location choice can lead to increased expenses, operational challenges, and limited scalability. This chapter delves into the key factors that influence site selection and explores strategic opportunities, such as leveraging edge networks to reduce latency, navigating regulatory environments, and future-proofing your data center for technological growth.

The Strategic Importance of Location in Data Center Development

LOCATION SELECTION is critical to data center development, affecting nearly every operational aspect, from the speed of data transmission to the facility's resilience against disasters. The right site can reduce operational costs, enhance performance, and support future technological advancements. Conversely, a poorly chosen location can incur significant costs and operational limitations, hampering your ability to remain competitive in a rapidly evolving digital landscape.

1. Proximity to Fiber Infrastructure

PROXIMITY TO EXISTING fiber optic infrastructure is one of the top considerations for selecting a data center site. Fiber optic networks are the internet's backbone, enabling high-speed data transmission over long distances. For a hyperscale data center, being near major fiber routes or Internet Exchange Points (IXPs) is crucial for several reasons:

- **Latency Reduction:** The closer a data center is to major fiber infrastructure, the lower the latency in data transmission. Low latency is critical for real-time applications such as high-frequency trading, video streaming, gaming, and real-time analytics.
- **Bandwidth Availability:** Proximity to robust fiber networks ensures the data center can handle large volumes of data traffic without bottlenecks, which is essential for cloud computing, AI, machine learning, and other data-intensive applications.
- **Redundancy:** Access to multiple fiber routes provides redundancy, ensuring continuous operation during a network failure. Redundancy is key to maintaining high availability and reliability, crucial for any hyperscale data center.

Case Example: A financial services company selected a data center location near a major IXP in New York City, significantly reducing latency for high-frequency trading applications. This strategic location choice allowed the firm to execute trades milliseconds faster than competitors, giving them a critical edge in the market.

2. Utility Availability and Cost

UTILITY AVAILABILITY, particularly electricity, is another critical factor. Hyperscale data centers consume vast amounts of power, so the availability, reliability, and cost of electricity are paramount considerations.

- **Power Supply Reliability:** A stable and reliable power grid is essential. Proximity to power generation facilities—such as hydroelectric plants, solar farms, or nuclear power stations—can enhance reliability. For example, a data center in Oregon was strategically located near hydroelectric power plants to ensure consistent power supply and minimize outage risks.
- **Cost of Electricity:** Electricity costs vary significantly by region. Choosing a location with lower electricity rates can result in substantial savings over the data center's lifespan. Sites near renewable energy sources often offer competitive rates and align with sustainability goals.
- **Scalability of Power:** The selected site must accommodate future growth. This may include options for adding additional transformers, substations, or backup generators.

3. Geographical and Climatic Considerations

THE GEOGRAPHICAL LOCATION impacts a data center's cooling requirements, disaster resilience, and overall operational efficiency.

- **Climate and Cooling Efficiency:** Cooler climates reduce the need for energy-intensive cooling, lowering operational costs. Data centers in warmer regions may require advanced cooling technologies like liquid cooling or air economization to maintain efficiency.
- **Natural Disaster Risk:** The risk of natural disasters—such as earthquakes, floods, hurricanes, and wildfires—should be carefully evaluated. Sites in disaster-prone areas must invest in resilience measures, such as reinforced structures, flood defenses, and redundant power supplies.
- **Topography and Soil Stability:** The physical characteristics of the land, such as topography and soil stability, play a crucial role. Stable soil and low seismic activity minimize the risk of structural damage. Additionally, flat or gently sloping land is generally more cost-effective for construction.

Case Example: A tech company located its data center in a region with a cool climate and low seismic activity, significantly reducing cooling costs and minimizing the risk of natural disasters. This decision improved operational efficiency and reduced insurance premiums.

4. Regulatory Environment

UNDERSTANDING AND NAVIGATING the regulatory environment is a crucial aspect of site selection. Different regions have various regulations affecting data center construction and operation.

- **Zoning and Land Use Regulations:** Ensure the land is zoned for industrial or commercial use and free from restrictions that might prevent data center construction. For example, a site in Texas was chosen because of its flexible zoning laws and streamlined permitting process, which expedited development.
- **Environmental Regulations:** Environmental regulations may govern energy consumption, emissions, water usage, and waste management. Compliance is a legal obligation and essential for sustainability and public perception. Sites in regions with stringent regulations may require additional investment in green technologies.
- **Tax Incentives and Subsidies:** Many regions offer incentives, such as property tax reductions, energy tax credits, and grants for infrastructure improvements. For instance, a data center in Virginia benefited from significant tax incentives, reducing upfront costs and improving the project's financial feasibility.

5. Cost and Availability of Land

THE AVAILABILITY AND cost of land are fundamental considerations, especially given the large footprint required for hyperscale facilities.

- **Availability of Large Parcels:** Finding large plots in urban areas can be challenging. Alternative strategies, such as multi-story designs or repurposing existing buildings, can maximize space utilization and reduce costs.

- **Cost of Land:** Land costs vary widely and impact the overall project budget. High costs in metropolitan areas may require creative solutions, like building vertically or selecting sites in less populated regions.
- **Hub Zones and Economic Opportunity Zones:** Locations in designated Hub Zones or Economic Opportunity Zones offer financial advantages, such as tax breaks or grants, making them attractive options.
- **Repurposing Existing Buildings:** Repurposing abandoned factories, warehouses, or commercial properties can offer faster development timelines, lower costs, and pre-existing zoning and infrastructure, reducing regulatory hurdles and environmental impact.

Example: A data center developer in Dallas repurposed an abandoned factory, cutting development costs by 30% and reducing the timeline to operational status by six months.

6. Accessibility and Community Impact

THE SITE'S ACCESSIBILITY and its impact on the surrounding community are critical factors.

- **Accessibility for Construction and Operations:** Proximity to transportation routes is crucial for logistics, but the site should also be far enough from residential areas to minimize disruptions, noise complaints, and security risks.
- **Community Impact and Engagement:** Engage with the local community early to demonstrate benefits and

address concerns, such as traffic, noise, and environmental impact. A data center project in Ireland included a public relations campaign emphasizing local job creation and economic benefits, which helped gain community support.

6. Future Expansion and Flexibility

FUTURE EXPANSION AND adaptability are essential when selecting a site.

- **Scalability for Growth:** The site should allow for future expansion, whether through additional construction phases or vertical growth. This flexibility is critical to accommodate emerging technologies and increased demand.
- **Flexible Design Opportunities:** Sites with open layouts or minimal zoning restrictions enable innovative design approaches, such as modular and containerized facilities.

8. Edge Networks and Latency Reduction

IN TODAY'S DIGITAL economy, speed is a competitive advantage, and latency is a critical concern.

- **Role of Edge Networks:** Edge networks are smaller data centers near end-users, designed to reduce latency by processing data locally before sending it to the central data center. This is crucial for industries like finance, gaming, and video streaming.

- **Integration with Hyperscale Data Centers:** While edge networks handle real-time processing, the central hyperscale data center manages long-term data storage and large-scale processing. Strategic location choices ensure seamless integration with edge facilities.

9. Access to Skilled Labor

THE AVAILABILITY OF skilled labor is vital for both the construction and operational phases.

- **Proximity to Tech Hubs:** Data centers require a workforce skilled in IT, engineering, construction, and maintenance. Being near tech hubs or universities ensures access to a qualified labor pool.
- **Training and Development Opportunities:** Regions with robust training programs or partnerships with educational institutions provide ongoing development opportunities for data center staff, supporting technological advancements.

10. Community and Economic Impact

THE DEVELOPMENT OF a hyperscale data center significantly impacts the local community and economy.

- **Job Creation:** Data centers create jobs during construction and operation. Engaging the community early helps build support and addresses concerns.
- **Infrastructure Development:** The presence of a data center can lead to improvements in roads, utilities, and

telecommunications, benefiting the broader community.

- **Community Engagement:** Proactively engaging with stakeholders, including government officials, business leaders, and residents, ensures the data center is seen as a positive addition to the community.

11. Assessing Project Feasibility

CONDUCT A THOROUGH feasibility study to determine the overall viability of the project, considering risks, costs, benefits, and success likelihood.

- **Market Analysis:** Evaluate the demand for data center services in the target region, the competitive landscape, and potential growth opportunities.
- **Financial Feasibility:** Analyze total ownership costs, including land acquisition, construction, utilities, taxes, and operational expenses, against projected revenues.
- **Risk Assessment:** Identify potential risks, such as regulatory changes, environmental concerns, supply chain disruptions, and geopolitical factors, and develop mitigation strategies.
- **Stakeholder Analysis:** Engage key stakeholders to gauge support for the project and identify potential obstacles.

The Strategic Importance of Location

CHOOSING THE RIGHT site for a hyperscale data center or any project is a complex decision with long-term implications. The ideal location enhances performance, reduces costs, and positions the data center for future growth and technological advancements. Conducting a comprehensive feasibility study and evaluating all relevant factors ensures the facility is operationally efficient and strategically positioned for success in an increasingly digital world.

Let's transition

WITH THE LOCATION SELECTED, the next step is to secure the site and assess potential environmental impacts. The following chapter will discuss the acquisition process, whether through purchasing existing buildings or developing new sites, and explore the importance of conducting thorough environmental impact assessments to ensure long-term viability and sustainability.

Chapter 3: Site Acquisition

ACQUIRING A GREAT SITE is one of the most critical steps in developing a hyperscale data center. The selection and acquisition of land or an existing structure will lay the foundation for the entire project. This chapter explores the various aspects of site acquisition, from selecting suitable land to negotiating the purchase and navigating the complexities of legal, regulatory, and environmental considerations. Given the increasing scarcity of large plots of undeveloped land, especially in metropolitan areas, repurposing existing buildings has become an attractive option. We will delve into these topics and provide practical guidance on ensuring a smooth and successful acquisition process.

Criteria for Selecting Suitable Land

FINDING THE RIGHT LAND for a hyperscale data center is a complex task that requires careful consideration of several key factors:

1. **Size and Scalability**
   The land must be large enough to accommodate the current data center infrastructure and any future expansions. Hyperscale data centers often require hundreds of acres, which can be challenging to find in urban or suburban areas. In these cases, consider building up instead of out—multi-floor hyperscale data centers are becoming increasingly popular and can be more cost-effective. This approach maximizes land use in areas where space is at a premium, reducing costs related to land acquisition and infrastructure development.
2. **Proximity to Power and Connectivity**
   The site should be close to high-capacity power lines and

fiber optic networks to meet the data center's energy and connectivity demands. While remote areas may offer more space, they might lack the necessary infrastructure, leading to higher costs for extending power and network services. Additionally, proximity to renewable energy sources, such as wind or solar farms, should be considered to enhance sustainability efforts.

- **Consideration:** Balance the availability of space with the cost of extending infrastructure. Proximity to diverse energy sources and strong network connectivity is crucial for minimizing latency and ensuring reliable operations.

3. **Environmental Considerations**
   Selecting land with minimal environmental constraints is crucial to avoid costly delays and legal challenges. Consider the following:
   - **Flood Risks:** Avoid areas prone to flooding or with a high-water table, as they pose significant operational risks and can lead to increased insurance premiums.
   - **Protected Habitats:** Ensure that the land does not encroach on protected wildlife habitats or contain endangered species, as this can lead to legal challenges, delays, and additional mitigation costs. (Don't overlook this!)
   - **Hazardous Waste:** Conduct thorough environmental assessments to confirm the site is free from hazardous materials like asbestos, lead, or other contaminants that could complicate development and require costly remediation.

4. **Zoning and Permitting**
   The land must be appropriately zoned for industrial or commercial use. Regions with favorable zoning laws and streamlined permitting processes can save significant time and reduce the risk of complications. Engage local experts to navigate zoning laws, understand any specific local restrictions, and secure the necessary permits efficiently.
5. **Accessibility and Security**
   The site should be easily accessible for construction, maintenance, and emergency services while also being secure enough to protect against unauthorized access and potential threats. Proximity to major transportation routes is essential for logistics, but the site should be far enough from residential areas to minimize disruptions, noise complaints, and security risks.

Repurposing Existing Buildings (Justin's note's: This is something I personally push to clients looking to be closer to the center of a city)

GIVEN THE SCARCITY of large, undeveloped plots of land, repurposing existing buildings has become an increasingly viable strategy for site acquisition. This approach offers several benefits:

1. **Faster Development Timeline**
   Acquiring an existing building, such as an abandoned factory, supermarket, or school, can significantly shorten the time required to bring a data center online. Much of the necessary infrastructure, such as power connections and basic structural elements, may already be in place,

reducing the need for extensive construction.

2. **Cost Savings**
   Repurposing an existing building can be more cost-effective than purchasing and developing raw land, particularly when the building has been vacant for some time. Sellers may be more willing to negotiate favorable terms, especially if the building is considered a liability.
3. **Zoning and Permitting Advantages**
   Existing buildings are often already zoned for commercial or industrial use, simplifying the permitting process. Local governments may be more inclined to approve projects that bring new life to vacant properties, particularly if they contribute to local economic development or urban renewal efforts.
4. **Sustainability and Environmental Impact**
   Repurposing a building can reduce the environmental impact of the data center project by minimizing the need for new construction materials and resources. This approach helps to revitalize areas that might otherwise remain underutilized, contributing to urban renewal and sustainability goals. Additionally, repurposing can help achieve green building certifications, such as LEED, by emphasizing reuse and recycling.

Challenges to Consider

WHILE REPURPOSING EXISTING buildings offers many advantages, it is not without its challenges:

- **Structural Support:** The building's structure must be capable of supporting the heavy loads and high energy demands of a data center, including the weight of racks, equipment, and cooling systems.

- **Retrofitting Costs:** Upgrading older buildings with modern cooling, power, and networking infrastructure can be complex and costly. Unexpected issues like asbestos, lead, or other hazardous materials can significantly increase project costs and timelines.

Negotiation Strategies and Legal Considerations

WHEN ACQUIRING LAND or an existing building, effective negotiation and a solid legal framework are essential to ensure a smooth acquisition process:

1. **Assessing Value and Potential**
   Conduct thorough due diligence to assess the value and potential of the property. This includes environmental assessments, structural evaluations, and a review of local market conditions. Don't assume that clients will flock to a site just because it's in a prime location; every aspect of the site's viability must be carefully considered.
2. **Flexibility and Contingencies**
   Negotiations should account for potential contingencies, such as additional infrastructure upgrades, unforeseen regulatory hurdles, or unexpected environmental issues. Include flexible terms in the contract to protect against delays, cost overruns, or changes in project scope.
   - **Side Note:** Soil samples are crucial, especially if the land is vacant. Issues like naturally occurring asbestos, old cemeteries, or other hazardous waste can render the land unusable or cause cost overruns. These factors should be discussed in the contract, with exit clauses for unforeseen issues. Don't assume your legal team will do this! Read the contract before sending it.
3. **Legal Framework**
   Ensure the legal framework is robust by:
   - Verifying clear title to the property.
   - Understanding any easements, covenants, or restrictions that may affect the development.

- Complying with all local, state, and federal regulations.

  Work with experienced legal counsel to navigate these complexities and draft contracts that protect your interests.

Environmental Impact Assessment

BUILDING A HYPERSCALE data center involves more than just finding the right piece of land or repurposing an existing structure—it also requires understanding and mitigating the environmental and community impact of the project. A comprehensive Environmental Impact Assessment (EIA) ensures that the data center is built responsibly and sustainably.

Conducting a Thorough Environmental Study

AN EIA IDENTIFIES, predicts, and evaluates the potential environmental effects of the proposed project before construction begins. Here's what a comprehensive EIA should include:

- **Baseline Environmental Conditions:** Assess the current state of the environment at the proposed site, including air and water quality, soil conditions, biodiversity, and existing land use.
- **Potential Environmental Impacts:** Evaluate the potential impacts of the data center, such as changes in land use, habitat disruption, water usage, emissions from construction and operation, and waste generation.
- **Cumulative Impacts:** Consider the cumulative impacts

of the data center in conjunction with other nearby developments.

- **Social and Economic Impacts:** Assess the social and economic impacts, including job creation and economic growth, as well as potential negative effects like increased traffic, noise, or strain on local infrastructure.

Mitigation Strategies for Minimizing Environmental Impact

ONCE THE POTENTIAL environmental impacts have been identified, develop strategies to mitigate these effects:

- **Site Selection and Design:** Choose a site that minimizes environmental disruption and design the data center to integrate with the natural landscape.
- **Energy Efficiency:** Implement energy-efficient technologies and renewable energy sources to reduce the data center's carbon footprint.
- **Water Management:** Use water-efficient cooling technologies, recycle water on-site, and source water from sustainable sources.
- **Waste Management:** Develop waste management practices that include recycling construction materials, reducing electronic waste, and managing hazardous waste responsibly.
- **Biodiversity Protection:** Implement measures to protect biodiversity, particularly if the site is home to protected species or critical habitats.

Community Impact and Engagement

BUILDING A DATA CENTER close to a town or city can bring both opportunities and challenges. While the economic benefits, such as job creation and increased local spending, can be significant, it's important to consider potential downsides and engage with the community throughout the planning process.

1. **Job Creation and Economic Benefits**
   Data centers often create jobs, both during construction and throughout ongoing operations. Emphasizing these benefits can help build community support. Engage local workforce development programs and collaborate with educational institutions to provide training and employment opportunities.
2. **Traffic and Infrastructure Strain**
   Large-scale construction projects like data centers can increase traffic, both during construction and operation. Mitigation strategies might include:
   - Improving local roads.
   - Scheduling deliveries during off-peak hours.
   - Providing transportation options for workers to reduce traffic congestion.
3. **Light and Noise Pollution**
   Data centers often operate 24/7, resulting in potential light and noise pollution. Mitigation strategies may include:
   - Using directional lighting to minimize light spillage.
   - Implementing noise barriers or soundproofing

solutions.
    - Designing the facility to minimize operational noise.
4. **Visual and Aesthetic Impact**
   The visual impact of a data center on the surrounding landscape can be a significant concern for local communities. To address these concerns:
    - Incorporate landscaping and green spaces.
    - Use color schemes that blend with the local environment.
    - Design low-profile buildings to reduce the visual footprint.

Permitting and Approvals

THE PERMITTING AND approvals process is a critical step in the development of a hyperscale data center. This process can be complex and time-consuming, varying significantly depending on the location and scale of the project. Successfully obtaining the necessary permits and approvals requires a strategic approach:

The Permit Process

SECURING PERMITS INVOLVES approvals from various local, state, and sometimes federal agencies. These permits cover everything from land use and building construction to environmental compliance and operational safety.

- **Understanding Local Requirements:** Thoroughly research local zoning laws, building codes, environmental regulations, and specific requirements related to energy usage, water management, and waste disposal.

- **Early Engagement with Regulators:** Engage with local authorities early in the planning process to identify potential issues and make necessary adjustments to the project plan.
- **Comprehensive Documentation:** Prepare thorough, accurate, and compliant documentation to facilitate a smooth permitting process.

Engaging with Local Authorities and Stakeholders

BUILDING POSITIVE RELATIONSHIPS with local authorities, community leaders, and stakeholders is essential for the success of the project.

- **Building Relationships with Local Authorities:** Maintain regular communication, demonstrate transparency, and show a willingness to address concerns to build trust and facilitate smoother interactions throughout the permitting process.
- **Community Engagement:** Engage with the community early and often. Organize town hall meetings, open houses, or information sessions to provide a platform for open dialogue.
- **Public Relations and Community Involvement:** A strong public relations strategy can play a vital role in gaining community support. Consider sponsoring local events, contributing to local initiatives, and demonstrating the company's commitment to the

community.

So the Site Acquisition is ehh not the hardest thing to do...

SITE ACQUISITION IS a complex and multifaceted process that plays a critical role in the success of a hyperscale data center project. However, it's not the hardest thing to do so don't overthink it. Whether acquiring raw land or repurposing an existing building, it's essential to evaluate all options carefully, considering factors such as scalability, environmental impact, and community engagement. A thorough understanding of the site's potential, coupled with strategic negotiation and legal considerations, will ensure that the data center is built on a strong foundation.

With the site acquired and the environmental impact assessed, the next step is to focus on the design and engineering of the data center. In the following chapter, we will explore the foundational elements of data center design, including the integration of sustainability features, cutting-edge cooling technologies, and the importance of security and compliance.

Chapter 4: Design and Engineering

Designing and constructing a hyperscale data center is a complex process that requires balancing standardized approaches with the flexibility needed to adapt to unique site conditions and evolving technological requirements. While baseline designs help simplify and expedite the project, they must be tailored to meet specific local requirements, operational needs, and future growth strategies. This chapter explores the critical components of data center design and engineering, including sustainability, resilience, security, human factors, the integration of emerging technologies, industry certifications, and strategic considerations for power and equipment standards.

DESIGNING WITH FLEXIBILITY: Standardization vs. Customization

Baseline Design: Standardizing for Efficiency

A baseline design provides a standardized template that can be adapted to different sites and client needs, conserving time and resources while maintaining consistency across multiple locations.

- **Example Baseline Design:** A single-story, 300,000-square-foot data center providing 50 megawatts of power is a common model. This configuration serves as a flexible and scalable template suitable for various applications, such as cloud computing, enterprise data management, AI processing, and machine learning.

Layout Planning: Optimizing Space and Scalability

Effective layout planning is crucial for maximizing current operations and enabling future growth. The design should optimize space utilization, scalability, and flexibility while considering local building codes, climate, and existing infrastructure.

- **Space Utilization:** In regions with high land costs,

multi-story designs can maximize available space. In warmer climates, enhanced cooling systems and building materials that mitigate heat gain are critical for maintaining operational efficiency.

- **Scalability:** Ensure the design can easily accommodate growth, such as adding server racks or increasing power capacity. Modular construction techniques, like prefabricated server modules, allow expansion in stages without significant disruption.
  Justin's Note: Avoid using proprietary equipment and oddball voltages (e.g., 415 volts) when standard voltages like 480 volts are more commonly available and easier to integrate.
- **Flexibility:** Layouts should enable the efficient arrangement of server racks, cooling systems, and power units while allowing room for future adjustments or expansions. Utilizing digital twin technology can simulate different layout scenarios and optimize the design for both current and future needs.

Integrating Sustainability Features

Modern data center design prioritizes sustainability to meet environmental goals, reduce costs, and comply with evolving regulations. This involves balancing the benefits of green technologies with their costs, material lead times, and operational impacts.

Energy Efficiency

Implementing energy-efficient technologies is essential for reducing operational costs and minimizing environmental impact.

- **LED Lighting and Energy-Efficient HVAC Systems:** Use components that lower power consumption. *Justin's Note:* It might be obvious, but sometimes investing in higher-quality equipment that draws less power (e.g., a $150 light fixture that draws 1 amp versus a $100 fixture that draws 6 amps) pays off in the long run.
- **Renewable Energy Integration:** Incorporate on-site renewable energy sources, such as solar or wind, to reduce the carbon footprint. (Justin's note: There might be a tax incentive and or grants available. Since well I assume you will have a flat roof...It might be beneficial for everyone involved including the community.)
- **AI-Driven Cooling Systems:** Leverage artificial intelligence for dynamic cooling management, adjusting systems in real time based on data center activity levels and external environmental conditions.
- **Free Cooling and Geothermal Cooling:** Utilize outside air or underground temperatures for sustainable thermal management when conditions permit, significantly reducing the need for mechanical cooling. Justin's note: Geothermal is great but... if not done correctly the well for which you use may warm up. Speak to your contractor about the heat transfer as you may need two-four wells.)

Water Conservation

Data centers often consume significant amounts of water, particularly those using water-cooled systems. Reducing water use is a key sustainability effort.

- **Closed-Loop Cooling Systems:** Reduce water consumption by recycling water within the cooling process.
- **Air-Cooled and Waterless Cooling Alternatives:** Use air-cooled systems or advanced waterless cooling solutions, such as two-phase immersion cooling, where feasible to eliminate water use altogether.

Sustainable Materials

Utilizing sustainable materials reduces the environmental footprint of construction.

- **Recycled Steel, Low-VOC Paints, Sustainable Insulation:** Use materials that reduce environmental impact while maintaining structural integrity and safety.
- **Local Sourcing:** Source materials locally to reduce carbon emissions from transportation and support the local economy.

Green Building Certifications

Achieving certifications like LEED (Leadership in Energy and Environmental Design) or BREEAM (Building Research Establishment Environmental Assessment Method) validates the facility's sustainability efforts and enhances its marketability to environmentally conscious clients.

- **LEED Certification:** Focuses on energy efficiency, water conservation, and sustainable materials. While obtaining LEED certification can increase upfront costs due to higher material standards and longer lead times, it may be critical for clients in sectors like machine learning or government contracts where sustainability is a priority.

- **WELL Certification:** Concentrates on human health and wellness in building design. While not always essential for cryptocurrency mining, WELL certification could be valuable for attracting and retaining top talent in high-skill areas, such as AI and machine learning.

Data Center Building Rating Factors

Data centers are rated based on their reliability, redundancy, and fault tolerance, guiding infrastructure investment and operational decisions. The Uptime Institute's Tier system is the most widely used classification, categorizing data centers from Tier I to Tier IV.

- **Tier I: Basic Capacity**
    - *Pros:* Simple, low-cost design.
    - *Cons:* No redundancy; vulnerable to downtime.
    - *Suitable For:* Non-critical applications.
- **Tier II: Redundant Capacity Components**
    - *Pros:* Reduced downtime risk due to redundant components.
    - *Cons:* Susceptible to downtime during maintenance or certain failures.
    - *Suitable For:* Small to medium-sized businesses.
- **Tier III: Concurrently Maintainable**
    - *Pros:* High reliability; allows maintenance without downtime.
    - *Cons:* More complex and expensive.
    - *Suitable For:* Large enterprises or mission-critical applications.

- **Tier IV: Fault Tolerant**
    - *Pros:* Maximum reliability; can withstand major failures.
    - *Cons:* High cost and complexity.
    - *Suitable For:* Critical infrastructure, such as financial institutions and healthcare.

REDUNDANCY CONFIGURATIONS: N+1, N+2, and 2N

Understanding redundancy configurations is essential for building resilient data centers.

- **N+1 Configuration:** One extra component beyond the minimum required.
    - *Pros:* Basic fault tolerance.
    - *Cons:* Single points of failure exist.
    - *Suitable For:* Facilities requiring basic redundancy.
- **N+2 Configuration:** Two extra components, providing greater redundancy.
    - *Pros:* Can handle multiple failures.
    - *Cons:* Higher cost and complexity.
    - *Suitable For:* Environments with higher uptime requirements.
- **2N Configuration:** Fully redundant with two independent systems.
    - *Pros:* Maximum reliability and fault tolerance.
    - *Cons:* Extremely expensive.
    - *Suitable For:* Zero-downtime environments, such as healthcare or emergency services.

Engineering Requirements

Electrical Infrastructure: Power Reliability and Distribution

A robust electrical infrastructure is critical to ensure uninterrupted operations.

- **Redundancy Configurations:** Implement N+1, N+2, or 2N configurations to provide backup options.
- **Power Distribution Units (PDUs):** Efficiently distribute power to equipment.
- **Uninterruptible Power Supply (UPS) Systems:** Provide short-term power during outages until generators activate.
- **Backup Generators:** Must be adequately sized, regularly tested, and maintained to guarantee reliability.
- **Shift to Lithium-Ion Batteries:** Adopt lithium-ion batteries for higher efficiency, longer lifespan, and reduced environmental impact compared to traditional lead-acid batteries.
- **Voltage Selection:** Stick to standard voltages like 480 volts to avoid complications with equipment availability and integration, reducing lead times and ensuring smoother operations.

Cooling Systems: Managing Thermal Loads

Efficient cooling is essential for maintaining optimal operating conditions and preventing equipment failures.

- **Air Cooling:** A common method using cooled air to dissipate heat. Techniques like hot aisle/cold aisle containment enhance efficiency.
- **Liquid Cooling:** Uses water or other fluids to absorb and remove heat; more efficient for high-density data

centers.

- **Hybrid Cooling:** Combines air and liquid cooling for optimized performance.
- **Advanced Cooling Techniques:** Implement two-phase immersion cooling and AI-driven cooling systems for dynamic management of thermal loads.

Hot Aisle Containment (HAC) and Cold Aisle Containment (CAC)

Managing airflow is essential to improve cooling efficiency and reduce energy costs.

- **Cold Aisle Containment (CAC):** Encloses cold aisles to direct cool air to servers.
- **Hot Aisle Containment (HAC):** Encloses hot aisles to contain hot air, directing it back to the HVAC system.

Lifecycle Cost Analysis

Consider all costs, including construction, operation, maintenance, upgrades, and decommissioning, to ensure long-term financial sustainability. Incorporate digital twin technology to simulate and analyze these costs over the entire lifecycle.

Modular vs. Traditional Builds

Modular construction offers speed and scalability, while traditional builds may be better for custom needs. Evaluate both approaches based on project goals, including flexibility, future expansion, and cost management.

Software-Defined Infrastructure

Software-Defined Networking (SDN)

Enables dynamic, flexible network management to respond quickly to changing demands and reduce operational costs.

Virtualization

Optimizes physical resources, reduces hardware needs, enhances scalability, and supports future technologies like hybrid quantum-classical computing.

Human Factors and Ergonomics

Operational Workflow

Design should consider human factors, ensuring easy access to equipment, ergonomic workspaces, and safety. Incorporate natural lighting, noise control, and temperature regulation to improve employee wellness.

Training Facilities

Incorporate training areas to ensure staff are well-equipped to manage new challenges and technologies, including emerging areas like AI, robotics, and quantum computing.

Compliance Beyond Data Protection

Environmental Compliance

Ensure ongoing adherence to environmental regulations concerning emissions, waste, and energy use, including planning for carbon capture and utilization technologies.

Health and Safety Regulations

Design to comply with occupational health and safety standards to protect workers. Include safety features like emergency evacuation routes, fire suppression systems, and first-aid stations.

Security and Compliance

Physical Security Measures

- **Fencing, Surveillance, Access Control:** Secure perimeters and interiors.

- **On-Site Security Personnel:** For rapid response to incidents.
- **Biometric Access Controls:** Advanced biometric systems for preventing unauthorized access to sensitive areas.

Data Protection Compliance

- **Encryption, Retention Policies, Regular Audits:** Ensure data protection compliance with regulations like GDPR and CCPA.
- **Quantum-Safe Cryptography:** Prepare for quantum computing by adopting encryption methods resistant to quantum attacks.

Mitigating Socioeconomic Threats

- **NDAs, Operational Security, Insider Threat Monitoring:** Protect against emerging threats from both internal and external sources.

Vendor and Supply Chain Management

Supply Chain Resilience

Plan for resilience in sourcing materials and components to avoid delays and disruptions. Evaluate the use of advanced analytics for predicting supply chain risks and mitigating them proactively.

Documentation and Change Management

Implement robust documentation and change management practices to handle modifications transparently and efficiently. Utilize digital twin technology to simulate changes and understand their impact before implementation.

Building for the Future

Security, compliance, and adaptability are key to the success of hyperscale data centers. By integrating cutting-edge technologies, adhering to rigorous standards, and proactively managing risks, data centers can remain resilient, efficient, and future-proof. The next chapter will explore best practices for vendor selection, contract negotiation, and ensuring that your data center project stays on track and within budget.

Chapter 5: Vendor Selection and Management

WHEN CONSTRUCTING A data center, vendor selection and management are among the most critical aspects of the project. Much like any large-scale construction effort, such as building a high-rise in Manhattan, the success of a data center hinges on the quality and reliability of the vendors involved. The importance of working with licensed and bonded—or at least bondable—vendors cannot be overstated. The stakes are high, and the consequences of vendor failure can be severe, leading to delays, increased costs, and even the potential for project failure.

A data center, at its core, is no different from any other complex construction project. Whether you're constructing a skyscraper or a state-of-the-art data center, the fundamental principles of construction apply. However, the specific demands of a data center require a specialized approach, especially when it comes to selecting and managing vendors. With current market conditions driving high demand for both vendors and materials, it's crucial to anticipate long lead times and challenges in securing reliable partners. Things can and will go wrong—vendors might fail to deliver or, worse, disappear halfway through the project. This is why it's essential to choose vendors who are not only capable but also bondable, ensuring your project stays on track despite any setbacks.

Avoid Proprietary or Non-Open-Source Solutions (Very important)

ONE KEY CONSIDERATION is to steer clear of proprietary or non-open-source technologies. Relying on such solutions can lock you into using a single vendor or material source, which can lead to inflated costs and limited flexibility. By opting for open-source and non-proprietary systems, you maintain vendor independence, control costs, and ensure that your data center can evolve with changing technology without being hampered by proprietary limitations.

Pitfalls to Avoid in Data Center Construction

TO FURTHER SAFEGUARD your project, here are some additional pitfalls to avoid:

Third-Party Project Management Companies

MANY THIRD-PARTY PROJECT management firms lack the necessary experience to manage data center construction effectively. Hiring these companies can result in unnecessary costs and inefficiencies. If your general contractor is capable and experienced, they should be able to handle project management, including tracking costs and ensuring timely completion. There's no need to incur extra expenses on third parties who may not add significant value and might only contribute to confusion.

Owner's Representatives Without Construction Experience

AVOID HIRING OWNER'S reps who don't have a background in construction. It's essential that those overseeing the project have hands-on experience—people who have actually "swung a hammer." Hiring reps without this experience can lead to poor decision-making and an inability to effectively manage the complexities of a construction project. Stick with professionals who understand the industry from the ground up.

Unqualified Newcomers and Scammers

THE BOOMING DATA CENTER market attracts many new companies, some of which may not be qualified or may even be outright scammers. These entities can jeopardize your project by providing substandard work or failing to deliver altogether. Remember, data centers are not mystical or inherently complicated to build; they require the same diligence and vetting as any other construction project. Avoid additional costs by selecting only experienced and reputable vendors.

Longevity Doesn't Guarantee Reliability

WHILE IT'S COMMON TO assume that a contractor who has been in business for many years is reliable, longevity alone does not prove their competence or trustworthiness. Some contractors and vendors manage to operate for long periods without being exposed for poor practices or even fraudulent behavior. A contractor might have a long history, but that history needs to be scrutinized for quality, ethics, and consistency. There are many examples where long-standing businesses have suddenly been exposed as fraudulent or have delivered subpar work under the radar for years.

Thus, it's important to dig deeper into a vendor's history, looking beyond just the number of years they've been in business. Investigate their track record, seek out client testimonials, check for any legal disputes or unresolved issues, and verify their performance on recent projects. Longevity is just one piece of the puzzle; reliability, ethics, and proven results are far more critical.

Licensed and Bonded Vendors: A Non-Negotiable

Requirement

IN THE CONSTRUCTION industry, working with licensed and bonded vendors is a standard practice designed to mitigate risk. Licensing ensures that the vendor has met specific professional standards and is legally permitted to perform the work. Bonding, on the other hand, provides a financial guarantee that the vendor will fulfill their contractual obligations. This is particularly important in data center construction, where the complexity and scale of the project can expose the owner to significant financial risk if a vendor fails to deliver.

Bondable vendors, while not always fully bonded at the outset, should have the financial stability and credibility to obtain bonds when necessary. This is crucial because, in a project as complex as a data center, vendors may need to secure additional bonds as the project progresses, particularly for high-value tasks or when dealing with critical path items.

The Importance of Qualified Vendors

JUST LIKE IN HIGH-RISE construction, the vendors working on a data center project must be qualified. This means they need to have the necessary experience, skills, and certifications to perform their specific roles. However, qualifications go beyond just having the right paperwork. A qualified vendor must also demonstrate a deep understanding of the construction process, the ability to work within the unique constraints of a data center environment, and a commitment to quality and safety.

In the context of data centers, certain vendors—such as those handling electrical installations, cooling systems, and IT infrastructure—need to be particularly skilled. The tolerance for error in these areas is minimal, as even a small mistake can lead to significant operational issues down the line. Therefore, it's essential to vet vendors thoroughly, ensuring they have a proven track record of success in similar projects or can adapt to your project's needs.

Teachable Vendors and the Learning Curve

WHILE IT'S CRUCIAL to work with qualified vendors, it's also important to recognize that not every vendor will have prior experience in data center construction. This is especially true as the demand for data centers grows and new vendors enter the market. In such cases, the vendor's ability to learn and adapt becomes a key factor in their selection.

The learning curve associated with data center construction is real, but it's not insurmountable. Many of the materials and technologies used in data centers—such as advanced cooling systems, high-density cabling, and redundant power supplies—may be unfamiliar to vendors who have not previously worked in this environment. However, with proper guidance and a willingness to learn, these vendors can quickly get up to speed.

The key is to select vendors who are not only qualified but also teachable. This means looking for partners who are open to learning new techniques, adopting new technologies, and working closely with the project team to ensure that all aspects of the data center are built to the required specifications. A teachable vendor is one who sees the learning curve not as an obstacle but as an opportunity to grow and expand their expertise.

Managing the Learning Curve

MANAGING THE LEARNING curve is a critical aspect of vendor management in data center construction. This involves providing the necessary training and support to ensure that all vendors understand the specific requirements of the project. It also means setting realistic expectations and building in time for the learning process within the project schedule.

One effective strategy for managing the learning curve is to pair less experienced vendors with those who have a proven track record in data center construction. This mentorship approach allows newer vendors to learn from the experience of others, reducing the risk of mistakes and ensuring that the project stays on track.

Another important consideration is the use of detailed specifications and clear communication. By providing vendors with comprehensive documentation and maintaining open lines of communication, you can minimize misunderstandings and ensure that everyone is on the same page. Regular meetings, progress reports, and on-site inspections are all essential tools in managing the learning curve and ensuring that the project is completed to the highest standards.

Long Lead Times and Vendor Reliability

ONE OF THE CHALLENGES specific to data center construction is the long lead times associated with certain materials and equipment. In a high-rise building, you might face delays due to weather or permitting issues. In a data center, delays are often related to the specialized nature of the components being used. For example, custom-built cooling systems, high-capacity generators, and advanced networking equipment can have lead times of several months.

Given the current market conditions, where demand for vendors and materials is at an all-time high, these long lead times and challenges in finding reliable partners are amplified. This is why it's so important to work with reliable vendors who can commit to the project timeline and deliver on their promises. A vendor's ability to manage their supply chain and deliver materials on time is crucial to the success of the project.

This is where the importance of bonding comes into play. Bonded vendors are financially incentivized to meet their obligations, providing an additional layer of security for the project. However, if you can avoid specialty products such as a busway system to power your rows, you should consider underfloor outlets that can be easily swapped when needed. Simplifying your approach wherever possible can help mitigate the risks associated with long lead times.

Vetting and Selection Process

THE VENDOR SELECTION process for a data center project should be rigorous and methodical. It begins with identifying the key vendors required for the project, including construction firms, equipment suppliers, and technology partners. Each vendor should be evaluated based on their qualifications, experience, financial stability, and ability to meet the project's specific requirements.

The selection process should also include a thorough review of each vendor's previous work, including site visits to completed projects, interviews with past clients, and verification of licenses and certifications. Additionally, it's important to assess each vendor's ability to work collaboratively with other project stakeholders, as successful data center construction relies heavily on teamwork and coordination.

Once vendors have been selected, the management phase begins. This involves establishing clear expectations, setting performance metrics, and maintaining ongoing communication throughout the project. Regular progress meetings, site inspections, and detailed reporting are all essential components of effective vendor management. By closely monitoring vendor performance and addressing any issues as they arise, you can ensure that the project remains on schedule and within budget.

Vendor Performance Metrics and Key Performance Indicators (KPIs)

TO ENSURE THAT VENDORS are meeting expectations, it's important to establish clear performance metrics and KPIs from the outset. These metrics can include:

- **On-Time Delivery:** Tracking the vendor's ability to meet deadlines.
- **Quality of Work:** Assessing the workmanship and quality of materials or services provided.
- **Responsiveness:** Measuring how quickly vendors respond to issues or changes in the project.
- **Compliance with Specifications:** Ensuring that all work is performed according to the agreed-upon specifications

and standards.

Including these performance metrics in the vendor contracts can provide a clear framework for evaluating vendor performance throughout the project.

Dispute Resolution Mechanisms

GIVEN THE COMPLEXITY of data center projects, disputes between the project owner and vendors may arise. Including a section on dispute resolution mechanisms could be valuable:

- **Mediation and Arbitration:** Outline the steps for resolving disputes through mediation or arbitration before escalating to legal action.
- **Escalation Procedures:** Define a clear process for escalating issues within the vendor's organization and the project owner's team to ensure that problems are addressed quickly and at the appropriate level.
- **Penalties and Incentives:** Discuss the use of penalties for non-performance and incentives for exceeding expectations as a means to encourage compliance and high performance.

Vendor Training Programs

TO SUPPORT TEACHABLE vendors and ensure they meet project expectations, consider implementing formal training programs:

- **Onboarding Sessions:** Provide comprehensive

onboarding sessions that cover the unique requirements of data center construction.

- **Ongoing Education:** Offer ongoing education opportunities, such as workshops or online courses, to help vendors stay updated on the latest technologies and best practices in data center construction.
- **Certification Requirements:** Encourage or require vendors to obtain specific certifications relevant to data center construction, such as data center infrastructure management (DCIM) or IT-specific certifications.

Exit Strategy for Underperforming Vendors

EVEN WITH THOROUGH vetting, some vendors may underperform. Having an exit strategy is crucial:

- **Termination Clauses:** Include clear termination clauses in vendor contracts that allow for the removal of underperforming vendors without excessive penalties.
- **Transition Plans:** Develop transition plans to quickly replace underperforming vendors with minimal disruption to the project. This includes having backup vendors identified and ready to step in if needed.

Justin's side note here: Listen you will have vendors FAIL you can count on it. You should always have supplemental vendors on standby. You should also only pay based on a SOV and never pay ahead.

Documentation and Knowledge Transfer

AS THE PROJECT PROGRESSES, it's important to ensure that all vendor-related knowledge is well-documented:

- **Project Documentation:** Require vendors to provide detailed documentation for all work performed, including installation manuals, maintenance schedules, and as-built drawings.
- **Knowledge Transfer Sessions:** Organize knowledge transfer sessions between vendors and the operations team to ensure that all relevant information is handed over before project completion.

Communication and Collaboration Tools

EFFECTIVE COMMUNICATION and collaboration among all stakeholders are crucial for managing a complex project like a data center build. It might be helpful to discuss the tools and platforms that can facilitate this.

Project Management Software

INTRODUCE THE USE OF project management software that can track progress, manage tasks, and ensure that all parties are aligned. Tools like Asana, Trello, or more specialized construction management software like Procore can be invaluable. (Justin's notes: Use one platform to streamline the whole project. Also, it is important that all vendors are contractually obligated to use whatever platform you are mandating to be utilized. Even if it cost you money to buy the licenses/seats. It will be worth every penny when you need to track items, get a feel for the project, etc.)

Regular Stakeholder Meetings

STRESS THE IMPORTANCE of regular meetings with stakeholders, including vendors, to ensure that everyone is on the same page. These meetings should focus on progress updates, upcoming milestones, and any potential issues that need addressing.

Legal and Contractual Considerations

THE LEGAL FRAMEWORK surrounding vendor agreements is critical to protect the project from unforeseen issues.

Contract Terms

DETAIL THE IMPORTANCE of clear contract terms that outline the scope of work, deadlines, penalties for delays, and quality standards. This ensures that all parties are legally bound to meet their commitments.

Force Majeure Clauses

GIVEN THE POTENTIAL for unexpected events (e.g., natural disasters, pandemics), including force majeure clauses in contracts can protect both the owner and vendors from liabilities beyond their control.

Ongoing Vendor Relationships Post-Construction

THE CHAPTER DISCUSSES vendor management during construction, but it might be useful to touch on the importance of ongoing relationships with vendors after the project is completed.

Maintenance Contracts

DISCUSS THE VALUE OF securing maintenance contracts with key vendors, particularly those who supplied critical systems like HVAC or electrical infrastructure. This ensures that the data center remains operational and well-maintained.

Vendor Reviews and Feedback Loops

ESTABLISHING A PROCESS for regular vendor reviews and feedback can help maintain high standards and address any issues promptly. This can also strengthen the relationship with vendors for future projects.

Security and Compliance Monitoring

GIVEN THE SENSITIVITY of data centers, it's crucial to consider ongoing security and compliance monitoring in vendor relationships.

Vendor Audits

PERIODIC AUDITS OF vendors, especially those involved in security and IT infrastructure, can ensure compliance with the latest standards and regulations.

Background Checks

ENSURE THAT ALL VENDORS, particularly those with access to sensitive areas, undergo thorough background checks to mitigate insider threats.

The Bottom Line: Simplicity and Clarity (KISS – Keep It Simple, Stupid)

IN CONCLUSION, WHILE data center construction may involve some specialized materials and technologies, it's fundamentally no different from any other large-scale construction project. The key to success is simple: work with licensed, bonded, and qualified vendors who can meet the project's requirements. Choose vendors who are teachable and adaptable, ensuring they can handle the learning curve that comes with data center construction.

Stick to the KISS principle—Keep It Simple, Stupid—you can avoid many of the common pitfalls that often plague data center projects. Approach vendor selection and management with simplicity and clarity. Focus on building a team of vendors who are not only capable but also genuinely committed to the project's success. When you keep things straightforward and clear, your data center project is much more likely to proceed smoothly, on time, and within budget—just like any other successful construction project.

Chapter 6: Procurement and General Pre-Construction

THE PRE-CONSTRUCTION phase is crucial for the success of any hyperscale data center project. This stage involves developing a detailed plan that includes procurement strategies, site evaluations, design coordination, permitting, logistics, and safety measures. Effective planning in these areas significantly impacts the project timeline, cost management, risk mitigation, and overall success. In this chapter, we will cover the essential elements of pre-construction, providing a comprehensive approach to ensure your project transitions smoothly into the construction phase, minimizing risks and maximizing efficiency.

Developing a Procurement Plan: Timing and Cost Management

TIMING

Time is critical (in all aspects including life. Sorry if I got too deep for you) in the procurement process, particularly for components that can impact the project's schedule. Identifying long lead-time items—such as custom electrical switchgear, high-capacity generators, or specialized cooling systems—is essential early in the planning process. Placing orders for these key items well in advance, potentially months or even years before they are required on-site, helps avoid delays that could derail the entire project timeline.

Cost Management

Effective cost management goes beyond price negotiation; it includes the total cost of ownership—storage, transportation, and potential penalties for delays. Locking in prices early and negotiating favorable terms with suppliers protects the project from price fluctuations and budget overruns. Additionally, maintaining a contingency fund within the procurement budget helps manage unforeseen expenses, such as expedited shipping or alternative sourcing in case of supply chain disruptions.

Sourcing Strategy

DIVERSIFICATION OF Suppliers

To mitigate supply chain risks, diversifying sources for critical materials is a prudent strategy. This reduces dependency on a single supplier and minimizes the impact of potential disruptions. Building relationships with multiple suppliers and exploring alternative materials or technologies as backups ensures continuity if primary sources become unavailable. Diversification also strengthens negotiating leverage, preventing any single supplier from becoming indispensable to the project.

Avoiding Proprietary Equipment

Wherever possible, avoid proprietary equipment that locks you into a specific vendor. Proprietary solutions can lead to inflated costs and limited flexibility for future upgrades or expansions. Opting for open-source or industry-standard components gives you greater control over the procurement process and allows for switching vendors without significant additional costs.

Contract Negotiation and Terms

CLEAR AND DETAILED Contracts

Contracts should explicitly define the scope of work, delivery schedules, payment terms, and quality standards. Ambiguities can lead to misunderstandings and disputes; therefore, every detail must be clearly outlined. Detailed specifications and performance expectations ensure that all parties understand their responsibilities and the standards they must meet.

Inclusion of Penalties and Incentives

Incorporate penalties for delays and incentives for early or on-time delivery to ensure vendors meet their commitments. Penalties could include financial deductions for each day of delay, while incentives might involve bonuses for hitting key milestones ahead of schedule. These contractual elements motivate vendors to prioritize your project and adhere to agreed timelines.

Escalation Clauses

Include escalation clauses that allow for price adjustments based on changes in raw material costs or other market conditions. These clauses protect both parties from unforeseen economic shifts but should be negotiated carefully to ensure fairness. The clauses must specify the conditions under which price adjustments are permitted and the formula used to calculate those adjustments.

Advance Purchasing

Consider directly purchasing vital materials and equipment in advance, rather than relying solely on vendors. Securing critical items yourself ensures they are available when needed, reducing the risk of project bottlenecks. This strategy also allows for bulk purchasing discounts and stockpiling materials that may be subject to future shortages or price increases.

Supplier Relationship Management

BUILDING STRONG RELATIONSHIPS with Suppliers

Strong relationships with suppliers ensure reliable delivery and favorable terms. Regular communication, transparency about project timelines, and a collaborative approach to problem-solving lead to better pricing, priority service, and more flexibility during challenging times. A partnership mindset with suppliers can encourage them to prioritize your orders and provide additional support when needed.

Vendor Bonding and Insurance

UNDERSTANDING BONDING Requirements for Large-Scale Projects

In large-scale construction projects like hyperscale data centers, financial and operational risks are significant. Ensuring that all vendors and contractors are adequately bonded and insured is crucial.

Types of Bonds:

- **Bid Bonds:** Ensure that if a contractor is awarded the project, they honor their bid and enter into a contract. If the contractor backs out, the bond compensates the project owner.
- **Performance Bonds:** Guarantee that the contractor completes the project according to contract terms. If the contractor fails to perform, the bond provides financial compensation to the project owner to cover the cost of completing the work.
- **Payment Bonds:** Ensure that subcontractors, suppliers, and laborers are paid for their work, preventing liens on the property due to non-payment.

Bonding Capacity

Evaluate vendors' bonding capacity to determine their financial stability and ability to handle large projects. A high bonding capacity indicates that the vendor is financially sound and capable of fulfilling their obligations.

Benefits of Bonding

Requiring bonds adds a layer of financial security to the project, ensuring funds are available to cover costs in case of default and minimizing the risk of project delays or additional expenses due to non-performance.

Insurance Considerations for Risk Management

PROPER INSURANCE COVERAGE

Comprehensive insurance coverage protects the project from various risks, including accidents, natural disasters, and legal liabilities.

Types of Insurance:

- **General Liability Insurance:** Covers claims for bodily injury, property damage, and personal injury during the project.
- **Workers' Compensation Insurance:** Provides coverage for medical expenses and lost wages for workers injured on the job.
- **Builder's Risk Insurance:** Protects the property and materials during construction from damage caused by events like fire, vandalism, or natural disasters.
- **Professional Liability Insurance:** Covers claims related

to design errors, negligence, or omissions by architects, engineers, and other professionals involved in the project.

- **Umbrella Insurance:** Provides additional liability coverage beyond the limits of underlying policies, such as general liability or workers' compensation. This is crucial for covering large claims that exceed the standard policy limits.

Ensuring Adequate Coverage

Verify that all vendors and contractors carry adequate insurance coverage, with limits sufficient to cover potential risks associated with the project's scale and complexity. This protects against financial losses and legal liabilities.

Including Liquidated Damages in Contracts

PURPOSE OF LIQUIDATED Damages

Include liquidated damages clauses in contracts to protect the project's timeline and budget. These clauses serve as financial penalties that contractors must pay if they fail to meet specific project milestones or complete the work on time.

- **Compensate the Project Owner:** For losses incurred due to delays, including additional financing costs, lost revenue, and other expenses.
- **Motivating Contractors:** The threat of liquidated damages motivates contractors to stay on schedule and proactively manage their work.
- **Calculating Liquidated Damages:** Calculate these damages based on a realistic assessment of the potential

financial impact of delays, including costs related to delayed equipment installations, labor mobilization, and potential disruptions to the overall project timeline.

Risk Management and Contingency Planning

RISK MITIGATION

Identifying potential risks early is crucial for preventing issues that could impact project success. Develop a risk management plan with strategies to address common risks, such as vendor bankruptcy, supply chain disruptions, or regulatory changes. Regularly review and update this plan to prepare the project team for any challenges.

Contingency Planning

Contingency plans for critical path items are essential. For example, if a key vendor cannot deliver on time, having an alternative supplier or pre-ordered materials can prevent delays. Maintain a reserve of critical materials and pre-negotiate contracts with backup suppliers.

Detailed Site Evaluation

SITE SURVEY AND SOIL Testing

- **Geotechnical Surveys:** Conduct thorough geotechnical surveys to assess soil suitability for heavy construction, preventing costly issues like foundation settling or instability.
- **Environmental Assessments:** Identify potential concerns, such as contamination, endangered species, or flood risks, ensuring compliance with regulations and

avoiding delays.

- **Topographical Surveys:** Conduct detailed topographical surveys to assess elevation, slope, and natural features, impacting the design and layout of the data center.

Pre-Construction Planning and Design Coordination

DESIGN COORDINATION

- **Value Engineering:** Optimize costs without sacrificing quality or performance by systematically examining project functions and finding the most cost-effective solutions.
- **BIM (Building Information Modeling):** Use BIM to coordinate design, construction, and operations teams, identifying potential conflicts (e.g., electrical, HVAC, plumbing) before construction begins, reducing costly rework.
- **Constructability Reviews:** Ensure the design can be efficiently built within the constraints of the site, budget, and schedule. Identify potential issues early and develop solutions before construction starts.

Permitting and Regulatory Compliance

PERMITTING STRATEGY

- **Early Engagement with Authorities:** Engage with local authorities early to identify regulatory hurdles and secure necessary permits, including understanding building codes, zoning laws, and environmental regulations.

- **Permitting Timeline:** Develop a clear timeline for obtaining permits, factoring in potential delays. A dedicated team or consultant can streamline the permitting process.
- **Community Engagement:** Engage the local community early, especially if the project is in a populated area, to address concerns and build goodwill, smoothing the permitting process and reducing opposition.

Pre-Construction Mockups and Prototyping

MOCKUPS

- **Physical Mockups:** Build physical mockups for critical components or systems to test design and construction methods before full-scale implementation, identifying potential issues and refining the design.
- **Virtual Prototyping:** Use virtual prototyping to simulate the construction process, identify potential problems, and train construction teams for improved efficiency.

Logistics and Supply Chain Management

SITE LOGISTICS PLANNING

- **Staging Areas:** Plan staging areas to store materials, equipment, and tools near the construction site. Efficient logistics planning minimizes delays and ensures materials are available when needed.

- **Delivery Scheduling:** Coordinate delivery schedules to avoid congestion on-site and ensure materials arrive just in time for installation, reducing on-site storage needs and minimizing disruptions.
- **Transportation Considerations:** Evaluate site accessibility for transporting large or heavy equipment, including necessary road upgrades or permits for oversized loads.

Pre-Construction Safety Planning

SAFETY PLANNING

- **Safety Protocols:** Develop comprehensive safety protocols tailored to the specific risks of the data center construction site. Train all workers on-site and ensure compliance with OSHA or other relevant safety standards. (Justin's little side note here: I always tell my clients to sub the safety portion out due to liability and just the ever-changing rules that will vary state to state city to city. Get a local company and let them do their job.)
- **Emergency Response Planning:** Establish emergency response plans for medical emergencies, fire, and other incidents. Conduct regular drills to ensure all workers are familiar with the protocols.
- **Site Security:** Implement security measures during the pre-construction phase, including fencing, surveillance,

and access control, to prevent theft or vandalism.

Budget and Financial Planning

BUDGET VALIDATION

- **Cost Estimation and Validation:** Validate all cost estimates against current market conditions before construction, accounting for potential price escalations due to inflation, shortages, or supply chain issues.
- **Contingency Planning:** Establish a contingency budget for unexpected costs during pre-construction and construction phases. Allocate a percentage of the total budget as a contingency reserve.
- **Cash Flow Planning:** Ensure adequate cash flow throughout the pre-construction phase by coordinating payment schedules with vendors and contractors and securing necessary financing or lines of credit.

Scheduling and Milestone Planning

DETAILED SCHEDULING

- **Master Schedule**: Develop a detailed master schedule outlining all pre-construction activities, from design finalization to permitting, procurement, and mobilization. This schedule should define start and finish dates, identify dependencies, and highlight key deliverables. Regularly update the schedule as the project progresses to reflect actual versus planned performance.
- **Milestone Tracking**: Identify key milestones during pre-

construction, such as obtaining permits, completing site surveys, finalizing designs, and securing critical equipment. Track progress against these benchmarks to ensure the project stays on track and allows for early identification of potential delays.

- **Integrated Scheduling**: Integrate the schedules of multiple contractors, subcontractors, and suppliers into the master schedule to ensure coordination and prevent conflicts between different trades. This ensures all parties work in sync and are aware of interdependencies.

CRITICAL PATH METHOD (CPM)

- **Identify the Critical Path**: Use the Critical Path Method (CPM) to identify the sequence of dependent tasks that directly impact the project's completion date. The critical path represents the longest stretch of dependent activities and dictates the shortest time possible to complete the project. Any delay in these tasks will directly affect the overall project timeline.
- **Focus on Critical Tasks**: Pay special attention to tasks on the critical path, ensuring they are prioritized, closely monitored, and allocated sufficient resources to avoid delays. Regularly review the critical path to account

Scheduling and Milestone Planning

DETAILED SCHEDULING

- **Master Schedule**: Develop a detailed master schedule outlining all pre-construction activities, from design finalization to permitting, procurement, and mobilization. This schedule should define start and finish dates, identify dependencies, and highlight key deliverables. Regularly update the schedule as the project progresses to reflect actual versus planned performance.
- **Milestone Tracking**: Identify key milestones during pre-construction, such as obtaining permits, completing site surveys, finalizing designs, and securing critical equipment. Track progress against these benchmarks to ensure the project stays on track and allows for early identification of potential delays.
- **Integrated Scheduling**: Integrate the schedules of multiple contractors, subcontractors, and suppliers into the master schedule to ensure coordination and prevent conflicts between different trades. This ensures all parties work in sync and are aware of interdependencies.

Critical Path Method (CPM)

- **Identify the Critical Path**: Use the Critical Path Method (CPM) to identify the sequence of dependent tasks that directly impact the project's completion date. The critical path represents the longest stretch of dependent activities and dictates the shortest time possible to complete the project. Any delay in these tasks will directly affect the overall project timeline.
- **Focus on Critical Tasks**: Pay special attention to tasks

on the critical path, ensuring they are prioritized, closely monitored, and allocated sufficient resources to avoid delays. Regularly review the critical path to account for any changes in project scope or unforeseen challenges.

Manpower Scheduling

- **Develop Manpower Plans**: Create detailed manpower schedules that align with the master schedule and critical path. Determine the required number of workers for each phase of the project, including their specific roles (e.g., electricians, HVAC technicians, engineers). Ensure that the schedules reflect peak workload periods and allow for adequate coverage during critical tasks.
- **Adjust for Labor Availability and Skill Levels**: Consider the availability of skilled labor in the region and plan for any training or recruitment needs in advance. Ensure the workforce has the necessary skills for specialized tasks, such as high-voltage electrical work or advanced cooling system installation.
- **Coordinate with Contractors and Subcontractors**: Collaborate with contractors and subcontractors to synchronize their manpower schedules with the overall project plan. Regularly communicate any changes in the schedule that may affect labor requirements to prevent downtime or overstaffing.
- **Monitor and Optimize Labor Utilization**: Continuously monitor manpower utilization to identify opportunities for optimization. Adjust schedules based

on project progress, labor performance, and any unforeseen changes to ensure efficient use of human resources.

Schedule of Values (SOV)

- **Establish a Schedule of Values**: Create a Schedule of Values (SOV) that breaks down the entire project into manageable components, each assigned a specific cost. This document serves as the basis for progress payments to contractors and ensures that costs are aligned with completed work.
- **Align SOV with Master Schedule**: Ensure that the SOV is integrated with the master schedule to provide a clear financial framework for the project. Regularly update the SOV to reflect any changes in scope, materials, or labor costs, and use it as a tool for tracking expenditures against the project budget.

This approach ensures that the project remains on schedule, within budget, and adequately staffed, thereby reducing the risk of delays and cost overruns. Justin's thoughts: Also remember you can have another SOV that incorporates your buckets to overlay the master. Streamline everything!

Pre-Construction Meetings and Stakeholder Engagement

PRE-CONSTRUCTION MEETINGS

- **Kickoff Meetings:** Hold a pre-construction kickoff

meeting with all stakeholders, including contractors, designers, and suppliers, to ensure alignment on project goals, timelines, and responsibilities.

- **Regular Progress Meetings:** Schedule regular progress meetings during the pre-construction phase to address any issues, review progress, and adjust the plan as necessary.

Pre-Construction game plan

THE PRE-CONSTRUCTION phase of a hyperscale data center project is complex and multifaceted, requiring careful planning and coordination across all aspects of the project.

Chapter 7: Construction and Project Management

BUILDING A DATA CENTER, whether a massive hyperscale facility or a smaller edge network, is often perceived as an inherently complex and unique endeavor. However, data center construction follows the same fundamental principles as any large-scale construction project. The key to success lies in applying these principles while addressing the specific requirements of data centers, such as power distribution, cooling systems, and security measures. This chapter delves into the essential aspects of construction and project management, emphasizing the importance of pre-construction planning, effective management, quality control, risk mitigation, and safety protocols.

Pre-Construction Planning and Mobilization

Justin's side note: Pre-con is just as important as construction itself.

Assembling the Project Team

The first step in pre-construction planning is assembling a team of qualified professionals with experience in data center construction. This includes selecting a general contractor, key subcontractors, architects, engineers, and project management personnel. Careful vetting of these individuals and firms is crucial to ensure they have the necessary expertise. The success of the project largely depends on the competence and coordination of this team.

Establishing Clear Objectives

Setting clear, well-defined objectives is essential for guiding the project. This includes establishing timelines, budget constraints, quality standards, and safety requirements. All stakeholders should agree on these objectives, and they should be documented and communicated to everyone involved. These objectives serve as the roadmap for the entire project, ensuring that all parties are aligned and working towards the same goals.

Site Mobilization

Mobilization involves setting up the construction site, securing the necessary permits, and arranging for utilities and site access. This phase includes establishing temporary facilities such as offices, storage areas, and worker accommodations. Proper mobilization ensures that the project can proceed smoothly once construction begins, minimizing potential disruptions and delays.

Risk Management Planning

Identifying potential risks early in the project and developing contingency plans to address them is a critical component of pre-construction planning. This includes everything from weather-related delays to supply chain disruptions. A well-prepared team can anticipate problems and respond quickly to minimize their impact, reducing the likelihood of costly setbacks.

Phased Construction Approach

Data center construction is typically carried out in phases, each building on the previous one. This phased approach allows for better management of resources, more accurate tracking of progress, and the ability to address issues before they impact subsequent phases.

Site Preparation

- **Clearing and Grading:** The first phase involves preparing the site by clearing any existing structures, vegetation, or debris. Grading the land ensures a stable foundation and proper drainage, which are crucial for the long-term stability of the data center.
- **Utilities Installation:** Installing utilities such as water, sewer, electricity, and communications infrastructure is a critical early step. These systems must be carefully

coordinated to meet the data center's long-term needs.

- **Foundation Work:** Laying a strong foundation is essential for supporting the data center's structural load. This phase involves excavation, pouring concrete, and installing footings and pilings as needed. Precision is key, as the foundation must support heavy equipment and maintain stability over the data center's lifespan.

Infrastructure Development

- **Power and Cooling Infrastructure:** As the backbone of the data center, power and cooling systems must be installed early in the construction process. This includes setting up electrical transformers, backup generators, and HVAC systems. Integration with the building's design is crucial to ensure efficiency and reliability.
- **Networking Infrastructure:** The installation of networking infrastructure, including fiber optic cables, data cabling, and network hubs, should be planned in conjunction with the overall layout of the data center. Proper routing of these systems is critical for maintaining performance and scalability.
- **Security Systems:** Security infrastructure, including access control systems, surveillance cameras, and fencing, should be installed as part of the infrastructure phase. This ensures that the site remains secure as construction progresses and that critical assets are protected.

Building Shell Construction

- **Structural Framework:** The building shell, including the structural framework, walls, and roof, is constructed during this phase. The design must accommodate the unique requirements of a data center, such as high ceilings for cooling systems and reinforced walls for security.
- **Weatherproofing and Insulation:** Ensuring that the building is weatherproofed and properly insulated is critical for maintaining the internal environment. This includes installing roofing materials, sealing joints, and adding insulation to regulate temperature and humidity.
- **Interior Build-Out:** Once the shell is complete, the interior build-out begins. This phase includes the installation of flooring, interior walls, lighting, and other finishes. Special attention must be paid to the layout of server rooms, control centers, and other critical spaces to optimize functionality and efficiency.

Meetings and Coordination

Owner-Architect-Contractor (OAC) Meetings

OAC meetings are crucial for maintaining alignment among all key stakeholders. Regularly scheduled meetings (e.g., weekly or bi-weekly) are held to discuss project progress, address potential issues, and review upcoming milestones. These meetings should have clear agendas and documented minutes to ensure accountability and effective communication. They help prevent misunderstandings and keep all parties aligned with the project's goals and objectives.

FIELD MEETINGS AND Site Walkthroughs

Field meetings, conducted on-site, focus on daily operations, safety protocols, quality checks, and work progress. These meetings often involve the project manager, site supervisors, and key subcontractors. Site walkthroughs are essential for visually inspecting ongoing work, ensuring it meets design specifications and quality standards, and catching potential errors before they become costly problems.

Project Management Meetings

Regular project management meetings involve the project manager, site managers, and subcontractor representatives. These meetings should focus on schedule adherence, resource allocation, cost control, risk management, and other day-to-day operational concerns. They provide a forum for discussing progress, resolving bottlenecks, and keeping the project moving smoothly.

Managing and Reporting During Construction

Request for Information (RFI) and Submittals Tracker

An RFI and submittals tracker is crucial for managing and documenting the exchange of information between the project team and subcontractors. An RFI tracker helps clarify ambiguities in design documents, while a submittals tracker ensures that all products and materials meet specifications and approvals. Maintaining a clear communication trail prevents costly delays, misunderstandings, or deviations from the design intent.

Progress Billing

Progress billing ties payments to the completion of specific milestones, incentivizing timely and accurate work while protecting against overbilling or incomplete work. This approach helps identify potential issues early, allowing for prompt resolution before they escalate into larger problems.

Regular Reporting and Documentation

Establish a regular reporting schedule, including updates on progress, budget, and any issues that have arisen. These reports should be shared with all stakeholders to ensure transparency and allow for quick decision-making when problems arise. Utilizing standardized reporting software allows for centralized communication, real-time updates, detailed reporting, and impact analysis. Regular reporting also helps maintain accountability and keeps the project on track.

Project Management Best Practices

Critical Path Scheduling

Critical path scheduling is a vital tool for ensuring that the project stays on track. The critical path represents the sequence of tasks that must be completed on time for the project to meet its overall deadline. Any delay in these critical tasks will directly impact the project's completion date.

- **Identification of Critical Tasks:** Identify tasks that are critical to the project's timeline—those with no flexibility in their start or finish dates.
- **Monitoring and Adjusting:** Regular updates to the schedule are necessary to reflect any changes or delays. If a task on the critical path is delayed, immediate action must be taken to mitigate the impact.
- **Resource Allocation and Risk Management:** Focus resources on critical tasks and develop contingency plans for them to ensure they are prioritized and completed on time.

Schedule of Values (SOV) Integration

Integrating the project schedule with the Schedule of Values (SOV) is an efficient way to streamline the construction process.

- **Integration of Milestones:** Align project milestones with the SOV to link payments directly to the completion of specific tasks or phases. This approach ensures that work is completed before payment is made and provides a transparent method for tracking progress.
- **Enhanced Accountability and Communication:** Payments contingent upon meeting specific deadlines incentivize timely completion, improve communication among stakeholders, and prevent disputes.

Expanded Quality Control and Risk Management

Quality Control Inspections and Testing

- **Regular Inspections:** Conduct regular quality inspections throughout the construction process to ensure work meets the required standards. Inspections should be performed by both internal teams and external quality assurance professionals to provide an unbiased assessment.
- **Testing and Commissioning:** Before systems go live, they must be thoroughly tested and commissioned. This process ensures that all systems function as intended and that any issues are resolved before the data center becomes operational.

Risk Mitigation and Contingency Planning

- **Proactive Risk Assessments:** Conduct regular risk assessments throughout the construction process to identify potential issues before they become significant problems. Develop contingency plans to address identified risks, such as backup suppliers or alternative construction methods.

Safety Management Systems

Implementing Safety Protocols and Standards

Develop comprehensive safety protocols covering all aspects of the construction site. Regular training sessions should be conducted to ensure all workers are familiar with the protocols, and continuous monitoring should be maintained to ensure compliance.

Third-Party Safety Oversight

Hiring third-party safety vendors can ensure impartial safety assessments and enforcement. Neutral parties are more likely to enforce standards without internal biases, maintaining a safe work environment and ensuring that safety protocols are rigorously followed.

Managing Construction Site Hazards

Proactively identify and mitigate construction site hazards. Implement emergency preparedness plans and conduct regular drills to ensure that all workers are familiar with the protocols. By staying ahead of potential hazards, the project team can reduce the likelihood of accidents and ensure a safer working environment.

Coordination with Local Authorities and Regulatory Compliance

Continuous Engagement with Local Authorities

Maintain continuous engagement with local authorities to ensure regulatory compliance throughout the construction process. This includes regular inspections, adherence to local codes, and obtaining necessary certifications.

Backbone of a Successful Data Center Build

Construction and project management are the backbone of any successful data center build—or, once again, any project for that matter. By emphasizing pre-construction planning, adopting a phased construction approach, and maintaining rigorous management and reporting practices, you can navigate the complexities of the construction process and bring your data center project to completion on time and within budget. While every project presents its own set of challenges, diligent planning, careful vendor selection, and proactive management significantly increase your chances of success.

In summary, treat data center construction like any other large-scale project—apply the fundamental principles of construction, stay organized, manage risks effectively, and prioritize quality and safety at every step. With these strategies in place, your data center project is poised for success, delivering a high-performing facility that meets all operational and client expectations.

Chapter 8: Commissioning and Testing

COMMISSIONING AND TESTING: Bringing It All Together

The commissioning and testing phase of a data center project is where all the planning, design, and construction efforts converge to ensure that the facility operates as intended. This phase is crucial for verifying that all systems function correctly, safely, and efficiently. It is a multi-level process, each with its own scope and purpose, but also highly adaptable depending on client requirements and site-specific conditions. Additionally, effective collaboration with the Authority Having Jurisdiction (AHJ) during inspections is essential for the successful completion of the project.

Data Center Levels of Commissioning: A Comprehensive Overview

COMMISSIONING A DATA center involves a series of steps designed to test and validate the functionality of all systems before the facility becomes operational. These steps are typically organized into different levels, each focusing on specific aspects of the project. While these levels provide a generic baseline, the exact steps and procedures will vary significantly between clients based on their specific requirements, standards, and industry practices. Each client may have their own guidelines that dictate how commissioning should be approached, making no two commissioning processes exactly alike.

- **Level 1: Factory Acceptance Testing (FAT):**
  The initial level involves testing individual components and systems at the manufacturer's facility before they are shipped to the site. The goal is to ensure that each component meets the required specifications and

functions as intended. Common examples include testing generators, UPS systems, and HVAC units. TAQUE reports are often generated at this stage to document the quality and performance of the equipment before it leaves the factory. FAT helps prevent costly delays and issues that could arise during later stages of installation and commissioning.

- **Level 2: Site Acceptance Testing (SAT):** Once the components arrive on-site, Level 2 commissioning tests these systems again to ensure they were not damaged during shipping and that they function correctly in their intended environment. Site delivery inspections are a crucial part of this process, as they verify that all equipment has arrived in good condition and is ready for installation. This level also involves verifying that the installation was completed properly. During this phase, the actual torquing of bolts is performed to ensure all connections meet specified torque settings. Each torque action should be meticulously logged, detailing the location, torque value, and the technician responsible. This torque log becomes a critical part of the commissioning documentation, ensuring that all mechanical connections are secure and meet the required standards.
- **Level 3: Pre-Functional Testing (PFT):** At this stage, the focus is on verifying that individual systems are installed and configured correctly. This includes testing the integration of components, such as

ensuring that electrical systems are properly connected and that HVAC systems are ready for operation. Pre-functional tests are designed to confirm that all systems are installed according to design specifications and are ready for functional testing.

- **Level 4: Functional Performance Testing (FPT):** This level involves testing the entire facility as an integrated system. The goal is to simulate real-world operating conditions and verify that all systems work together as expected. Commissioning scripts are essential during this phase, as they provide detailed procedures and step-by-step instructions for testing each system. These scripts ensure that all necessary tests are performed consistently and thoroughly, minimizing the risk of oversight. Additionally, real-world simulations help identify potential issues before the facility becomes fully operational, ensuring a smooth transition to production.

Vendor and Subcontractor Preparedness: It's crucial for vendors and subcontractors to be fully prepared during this phase. This includes having all necessary equipment, such as load banks, readily available. Load banks are critical for testing power systems under load conditions to ensure they can handle the required capacity. In some regions, there may be specific restrictions or windows of time during which load bank testing can occur. For example, the local utility or grid operator might only allow an 8-hour testing window during nighttime hours, and certain months like August may be off-limits due to high power demand. These restrictions are often tied to the source of power and grid capacity, making it essential to plan testing schedules carefully to avoid conflicts and delays. Subcontractors must also ensure that they have adequately trained personnel on-site who are familiar with the commissioning scripts and testing protocols.

- **Level 5: Integrated Systems Testing (IST):**
  The final level of commissioning involves comprehensive testing of all systems under simulated operating conditions, including emergency scenarios like power failures or cooling system malfunctions. The purpose is to ensure that backup systems activate as required and to verify that the facility meets all performance criteria outlined in the design. It's essential to clarify with clients that these levels are part of a standardized commissioning process and are not interchangeable with the design scope. For instance, Level 1 commissioning, which involves factory acceptance testing, is not about confirming that a generator will work based on a design calculation; rather, it's about ensuring that the generator meets the manufacturer's specifications before it's shipped.

Third-Party Testing and Certification: The Role of Underwriters Laboratories and Others

IN ADDITION TO THE internal commissioning levels, third-party testing and certification play a vital role in ensuring the reliability and safety of the data center's systems. Engaging independent organizations, such as Underwriters Laboratories (UL), adds an extra layer of credibility and compliance to the project.

- **Underwriters Laboratories (UL):**
  UL is one of the most recognized independent testing organizations that certifies products and systems for safety and compliance with industry standards. In data

center construction, UL testing can be applied to electrical components, fire suppression systems, and other critical infrastructure. Having UL certification provides assurance that these systems meet stringent safety requirements and are less likely to fail during operation.

- **Other Third-Party Testing Agencies:** Depending on the project's scope and location, other third-party agencies might be involved in testing and certifying different aspects of the data center. These might include environmental testing, seismic certification, or energy efficiency ratings. Collaborating with these agencies during the commissioning phase ensures that the facility complies with all necessary regulations and performance standards.
-

AHJ Inspections: Navigating the Complications

THE AUTHORITY HAVING Jurisdiction (AHJ) plays a critical role in the commissioning and testing phase. The AHJ is responsible for ensuring that the data center complies with all relevant codes, standards, and regulations. Navigating AHJ inspections can be complex, and it's vital to establish a good working relationship with the AHJ early in the project.

- **Common Complications During AHJ Inspections:**
    - **Varying Interpretations of Codes:** Different jurisdictions may have different interpretations of building codes and safety

regulations. What is acceptable in one location might not be in another. It's important to understand the specific requirements of the AHJ in your jurisdiction and ensure that your design and construction meet those standards.

- **Documentation and Compliance:** The AHJ will require comprehensive documentation to verify compliance with codes and regulations. This includes drawings, specifications, test reports, and certifications. Ensuring that all documentation is complete, accurate, and readily available is crucial for a smooth inspection process.
- **Scheduling and Delays:** AHJ inspections must be scheduled in advance, and any issues identified during the inspection can lead to delays. It's important to build flexibility into your project timeline to accommodate these inspections and any necessary corrections.

- **Establishing a Good Working Relationship with the AHJ:**
    - **Early Engagement:** Engage with the AHJ early in the project to discuss the scope, schedule, and any potential challenges. This helps to set expectations and allows you to address any concerns before they become issues during the inspection phase.
    - **Open Communication:** Maintain open and transparent communication with the AHJ throughout the project. This includes providing regular updates on progress, addressing any questions or concerns promptly, and ensuring that all communications are documented.
    - **Proactive Problem Solving:** If issues arise during inspections, work proactively with the AHJ to find solutions. Demonstrating a willingness to address concerns and make necessary adjustments can help build trust and facilitate a smoother

inspection process.

- **Respect for Authority:** Always respect the authority of the AHJ. Their role is to ensure the safety and compliance of the project, and they have the final say in whether the facility can be approved for operation. Working collaboratively with the AHJ can help prevent conflicts and ensure a positive outcome.

Post-Commissioning Reviews, Audits, and Continuous Improvement

AFTER THE COMMISSIONING and testing phase is complete, conducting post-commissioning reviews and audits can provide valuable insights and help identify areas for improvement.

- **Post-Commissioning Reviews:** Evaluate the performance of systems over time to ensure they operate as expected under normal conditions. This can help identify any issues that may not have been apparent during the initial commissioning phase.
- **Third-Party Audits:** Independent third-party audits validate the effectiveness of the commissioning process and ensure ongoing compliance with industry standards and regulations. This is particularly important for data centers subject to strict regulatory requirements.

Integration with Existing Infrastructure

IF THE NEW DATA CENTER is part of a broader network or is replacing an existing facility, it's crucial to test how the new systems integrate with the existing infrastructure.

- **Integration Testing:** This includes testing network connections, software compatibility, and data migration processes to ensure seamless operation across the entire infrastructure.

Energy Efficiency and Sustainability Verification

VERIFYING THAT THE data center meets its energy efficiency and sustainability targets is an essential aspect of the commissioning process.

- **Energy Efficiency Testing:** Monitor energy use under different load conditions to ensure that cooling systems and other infrastructure operate efficiently. This testing helps confirm that the data center meets its design goals for energy use.
- **Sustainability Compliance:** If the data center has sustainability certifications or goals (e.g., LEED), additional testing and documentation may be required to ensure compliance with these standards.

Remote Monitoring, Automation, and Cybersecurity

AS DATA CENTERS INCREASINGLY rely on remote monitoring, automation, and robust cybersecurity, it's vital to ensure these systems are fully functional during commissioning.

- **Remote Monitoring and Automation:** Set up and test remote monitoring systems to ensure they provide real-time data on the facility's performance. Test automation systems to verify they control and optimize various aspects of the data center's operations.

- **Cybersecurity Considerations:** Conduct penetration testing and other security assessments to ensure the data center's systems are secure from cyber threats before becoming fully operational.

Documentation, Handover, and Lessons Learned

THE FINAL PHASE OF commissioning involves ensuring that all documentation is in order and that the operations team is fully prepared to take over the facility.

- **Comprehensive Documentation:** Provide detailed documentation, including as-built drawings, test results, operation manuals, and maintenance schedules. This documentation is critical for long-term management and maintenance.
- **Handover Process:** Implement a formal handover process, ensuring that all systems, documentation, and responsibilities are transferred smoothly to the operations team.
- **Lessons Learned and Continuous Improvement:** Gather feedback from all stakeholders to identify areas for improvement and document best practices for future projects. Encourage a mindset of continuous improvement, using the lessons learned to refine and optimize the commissioning process in future projects.

Commissioning and testing are critical components of the data center construction process, ensuring that the facility is ready for operation and meets all performance and safety standards. By understanding the different levels of commissioning, incorporating third-party testing and certifications like those from UL, and working effectively with the AHJ, you can navigate this phase successfully. It is also important to acknowledge the variability in commissioning procedures based on client requirements, including the use of commissioning scripts, the preparedness of vendors with necessary equipment like load banks, and the specific protocols for filling diesel tanks.

Additionally, post-commissioning monitoring, thorough training, and proper documentation set the stage for long-term success. Remember, commissioning is about more than just verifying that systems work—it's about ensuring that the entire facility operates as an integrated, reliable, and compliant system. Establishing a strong relationship with the AHJ, managing inspections, and incorporating lessons learned will help achieve a successful and timely project completion.

Chapter 9: Data Center Operations and Management

ONCE THE DATA CENTER is fully commissioned and handed over to the operations team, the focus shifts to the ongoing management and maintenance of the facility. Effective data center operations are critical to ensuring the reliability, efficiency, and security of the facility. This chapter covers the key elements of data center operations, including the establishment of standard operating procedures (SOPs), maintenance schedules, monitoring systems, and much more.

Establishing Standard Operating Procedures (SOPs)

STANDARD OPERATING Procedures (SOPs) are the backbone of effective data center management. SOPs provide detailed instructions on how to carry out routine operations, handle emergencies, and maintain critical systems. They ensure consistency, safety, and efficiency in day-to-day operations.

Developing SOPs:

SOPS SHOULD BE DEVELOPED for all critical aspects of data center operations, including power management, cooling systems, security protocols, and data management. These procedures should be detailed, easy to follow, and regularly updated to reflect any changes in technology or operational requirements.

Method of Procedures (MOPs):

IN ADDITION TO GENERAL SOPs, Method of Procedures (MOPs) should be established for specific tasks that require detailed, step-by-step instructions. MOPs are particularly important for complex operations such as system upgrades, maintenance activities, or emergency responses. They provide a structured approach to ensure that tasks are carried out safely and correctly, minimizing the risk of errors.

Emergency Procedures:

SOPS MUST INCLUDE CLEAR instructions for handling emergencies, such as power outages, equipment failures, or security breaches. These procedures should outline the immediate actions to be taken, the personnel responsible, and the communication protocols to be followed. Regular drills should be conducted to ensure that all staff are familiar with these procedures and can respond effectively in an emergency.

Training and Compliance:

ALL DATA CENTER STAFF should be trained on the SOPs and MOPs relevant to their roles. Regular refresher training should be provided to ensure that staff remain familiar with the procedures and any updates. Compliance with SOPs should be monitored, and any deviations should be investigated and addressed promptly.

Maintenance Schedules and Monitoring Systems

ONGOING MAINTENANCE and monitoring are essential for maintaining the operational integrity of the data center. These activities help to prevent system failures, extend the lifespan of equipment, and ensure that the facility operates efficiently.

Establishing Maintenance Schedules:

A DETAILED MAINTENANCE schedule should be established for all critical systems, including power distribution, cooling systems, networking infrastructure, and security systems. This schedule should be based on manufacturer recommendations, industry best practices, and the specific needs of the facility. Regular maintenance tasks may include inspections, cleaning, component replacements, and system tests.

Preventive vs. Predictive Maintenance:

PREVENTIVE MAINTENANCE involves regularly scheduled tasks aimed at preventing equipment failures, such as replacing worn components or cleaning filters. Predictive maintenance, on the other hand, uses data from monitoring systems to predict when equipment is likely to fail and schedule maintenance accordingly. Both approaches should be integrated into the overall maintenance strategy to maximize efficiency and minimize downtime.

Monitoring Systems:

CONTINUOUS MONITORING of the data center's systems is critical for detecting and addressing issues before they lead to failures. Monitoring systems should track key metrics such as power usage, temperature, humidity, network performance, and security alerts. Automated alerts should be set up to notify the operations team of any anomalies that could indicate a potential problem.

Condition-Based Monitoring:

CONDITION-BASED MONITORING involves using real-time data from sensors and monitoring systems to assess the health of equipment and systems. This approach allows for more targeted maintenance, focusing efforts on equipment that shows signs of wear or potential failure. Condition-based monitoring can help reduce unnecessary maintenance and extend the lifespan of critical systems.

Regular Audits and Inspections:

IN ADDITION TO ROUTINE maintenance, regular audits and inspections should be conducted to assess the overall condition of the data center. These inspections should review the physical infrastructure, evaluate compliance with SOPs, and identify any areas where improvements can be made. The results of these audits should be documented and used to inform future maintenance and operational strategies.

Operational Efficiency Metrics

OPERATIONAL EFFICIENCY is key to the success of any data center. Monitoring and improving Key Performance Indicators (KPIs) can drive efficiency and reduce operational costs.

Key Performance Indicators (KPIs):

- **Power Usage Effectiveness (PUE):** Measures the ratio of total facility energy to the energy used by IT equipment. A lower PUE indicates higher efficiency.
- **Data Center Infrastructure Efficiency (DCiE):** The inverse of PUE, it measures the percentage of energy used by IT equipment relative to the total energy consumed by the facility.
- **IT Equipment Efficiency (ITEE):** Evaluates the energy efficiency of the IT equipment itself, contributing to the overall energy efficiency of the data center.

Improving Efficiency:

- **Optimizing Cooling Systems:** Implement advanced cooling strategies, such as hot aisle/cold aisle containment, liquid cooling, or free cooling techniques.
- **Enhancing Server Utilization:** Use virtualization and dynamic resource allocation to optimize server usage, reducing energy waste.

Automation and AI Integration

AUTOMATION AND ARTIFICIAL intelligence (AI) are transforming data center operations, enabling more efficient management and faster response times.

Automation in Operations:

AUTOMATION CAN STREAMLINE routine tasks such as system monitoring, resource allocation, and incident response. AI can predict equipment failures, optimize energy consumption, and manage workloads more effectively.

Benefits of Automation:

- **Reduced Human Error:** Automation ensures consistent execution of tasks, reducing the likelihood of mistakes.
- **Improved Response Times:** Automated systems can react faster to issues, minimizing downtime and maintaining service levels.
- **Predictive Maintenance:** AI can analyze data from monitoring systems to predict when maintenance is needed, preventing failures and extending equipment life.

Change Management Framework

EFFECTIVE CHANGE MANAGEMENT is crucial for ensuring that updates to the data center's infrastructure are implemented smoothly and without disrupting operations.

Change Advisory Board (CAB):

ESTABLISH A CHANGE Advisory Board to review and approve all changes in the data center. The CAB should include representatives from operations, IT, security, and management to ensure that all perspectives are considered.

Communication Strategies:

CLEAR COMMUNICATION is essential during changes. Inform all stakeholders and the operations team about upcoming changes, including the timeline, expected impact, and contingency plans.

Incident Management and Root Cause Analysis (RCA)

INCIDENT MANAGEMENT and Root Cause Analysis (RCA) are essential for responding to issues and preventing them from recurring.

Incident Management:

ESTABLISH A STRUCTURED approach to identifying, responding to, and resolving incidents. This includes setting up an Incident Response Team (IRT) with clear roles and responsibilities.

Root Cause Analysis (RCA):

AFTER AN INCIDENT, conduct a Root Cause Analysis to understand the underlying cause and implement measures to prevent recurrence. RCA involves identifying the root cause, analyzing contributing factors, and documenting corrective actions.

Vendor Management and Security

MANAGING RELATIONSHIPS with vendors and ensuring robust security measures are in place are crucial for protecting the facility from both internal and external threats.

Master Service Agreements (MSAs) with Vendors:

A MASTER SERVICE AGREEMENT (MSA) is a contract that outlines the general terms and conditions of the relationship between the data center and its vendors. MSAs provide a framework for working with multiple vendors, ensuring that all parties understand their responsibilities and the expectations for service delivery.

Performance Metrics and SLAs:

WITHIN THE MSA, SPECIFIC Service Level Agreements (SLAs) should be defined. SLAs establish the minimum acceptable levels of service that vendors must meet, such as response times, uptime guarantees, and maintenance schedules.

Third-Party Vetting of Employees and Vendors:

TO MITIGATE THE RISKS of corporate espionage, security breaches, hackers, and other threats, all employees and vendors must undergo rigorous vetting by a trusted third party. This vetting process should include background checks, verification of credentials, and assessments of any potential security risks.

Scaling and Upgrading

AS TECHNOLOGY EVOLVES and business needs change, data centers must be able to scale and upgrade their infrastructure to keep pace. Planning for future growth and ensuring that upgrades can be performed with minimal disruption are key aspects of long-term data center operations.

Capacity Planning:

CAPACITY PLANNING INVOLVES forecasting future demand and ensuring that the data center has the physical space, power, and cooling capacity to support growth.

Modular Design:

IMPLEMENTING A MODULAR design approach can make it easier to scale the data center as needed. Modular components, such as prefabricated server modules or scalable power systems, can be added or upgraded without requiring a complete overhaul of the facility.

Technology Roadmap:

DEVELOPING A TECHNOLOGY roadmap is essential for planning upgrades and ensuring that the data center remains up-to-date with the latest advancements.

Strategies for Minimizing Downtime During Upgrades:

- **Redundant Systems:** Maintain redundant systems to ensure continuous operation during upgrades.
- **Phased Upgrades:** Plan and execute upgrades in phases to minimize disruption.
- **Scheduled Maintenance Windows:** Schedule upgrades during predefined maintenance windows, when the impact on operations will be minimal.
- **Backup and Recovery Plans:** Ensure comprehensive backup and recovery plans are in place before any upgrade.

Ongoing Compliance and Audits

MAINTAINING ONGOING compliance and conducting regular audits are essential practices for ensuring that a data center remains secure, efficient, and fully operational.

Regular Audits for Security and Regulatory Compliance:

- **Security Audits:** Conduct thorough security audits to review access controls, surveillance systems, and network security measures.

- **Regulatory Compliance Audits:** Ensure adherence to all applicable laws, regulations, and industry standards.
- **Frequency of Audits:** Perform audits regularly, with the frequency determined by the level of risk and specific requirements.
- **Documentation and Reporting:** Document all audit findings and share reports with key stakeholders.

Implementing Continuous Improvement Practices

CONTINUOUS IMPROVEMENT is an ongoing effort to enhance data center operations by identifying inefficiencies, addressing weaknesses, and implementing best practices.

Feedback Loops:

ESTABLISH FEEDBACK loops from regular audits, inspections, and daily operations to identify areas for improvement.

Process Optimization:

REGULARLY REVIEW AND refine operational processes, update SOPs, and adopt new technologies that improve efficiency.

Benchmarking:

BENCHMARK AGAINST INDUSTRY standards and best practices to measure performance relative to peers.

Training and Development:

INVEST IN ONGOING EDUCATION and professional development to keep the team current with the latest trends, technologies, and best practices.

Client Communication and Reporting

REGULAR COMMUNICATION with clients and stakeholders is vital for maintaining transparency, building trust, and ensuring the long-term success of the data center.

Client Reporting:

ESTABLISH A REGULAR reporting schedule to update clients on the status of the data center. This should include performance metrics, upcoming maintenance, and any incidents that have been resolved.

Sustainability Reporting:

INCLUDE REPORTS ON sustainability efforts to stakeholders, demonstrating a commitment to environmental responsibility.

Stakeholder Engagement:

ENGAGE WITH ALL STAKEHOLDERS through regular updates and meetings to ensure alignment on the data center's current status and future plans.

Technology Lifecycle and Change Management

EFFECTIVELY MANAGING the lifecycle of technology and ensuring that changes are well-documented and controlled are crucial for maintaining the data center's operational integrity and efficiency.

Technology Lifecycle Management:

- **End-of-Life Planning:** Plan for the retirement and replacement of outdated equipment.
- **Asset Management:** Implement asset management practices, including inventory management and tracking of hardware and software lifecycles.

Change Management:

- **Managing Change:** Establish a formal change management process to control and document changes.
- **Documenting Changes:** Maintain detailed records of all changes for future reference and compliance audits.

Disaster Recovery and Incident Response Planning

EFFECTIVE DISASTER recovery and incident response plans are essential for ensuring business continuity and protecting the data center from unexpected events.

Incident Response Plan:

DEVELOP A COMPREHENSIVE incident response plan that details how to handle unexpected events such as cyber-attacks, natural disasters, or major system failures.

Disaster Recovery Plan (DRP):

ENSURE THAT THE DATA center has a robust disaster recovery plan in place, including backup strategies, data restoration processes, and recovery time objectives (RTO).

Geographic Diversity in Disaster Recovery Sites:

PLAN FOR DISASTER RECOVERY sites that are geographically diverse to protect against regional disasters.

Energy Efficiency and Sustainability

SUSTAINABILITY IS BECOMING an increasingly important aspect of data center operations. Implementing energy-efficient practices and considering renewable energy sources can reduce costs and enhance the data center's environmental footprint.

Energy Management:

FOCUS ON OPTIMIZING energy use through energy-efficient hardware, optimizing cooling systems, and leveraging renewable energy sources.

Sustainability Initiatives:

ADOPT SUSTAINABILITY practices, such as reducing the data center's carbon footprint, improving waste management, and using environmentally friendly materials.

Renewable Energy Integration:

EXPLORE OPPORTUNITIES to integrate renewable energy sources, such as solar or wind power, into the data center's energy strategy.

So what have we learned here? Well we talked about data center operations and how they require careful planning, robust security measures, and the ability to adapt to changing demands. By establishing comprehensive SOPs, developing detailed maintenance schedules, and implementing robust monitoring systems, you can ensure that the data center operates smoothly and that any issues are identified and addressed before they escalate. Additionally, managing relationships with vendors, planning for future growth, and executing upgrades with minimal downtime are critical for maintaining the data center's competitive edge and ensuring its long-term success. Ongoing compliance, regular audits, and continuous improvement practices are essential for maintaining high standards of safety and uptime. Through these strategies, you can create a data center that is secure, scalable, and resilient in the face of evolving challenges.

Chapter 10: Case Studies

AS WE'VE EXPLORED THROUGHOUT this book, building and operating a hyperscale data center is a complex, multifaceted endeavor that requires meticulous planning, rigorous execution, and continuous oversight. Even with the best intentions and thorough documentation, things can slip through the cracks. At the end of the day, it's people dealing with people, and human error is inevitable. That's why thorough documentation and continuous learning are not just best practices—they're necessities.

This chapter delves into real-world examples of successful hyperscale data centers across different sectors, highlighting lessons learned and best practices that can be applied to future projects. Remember, you can document all the "lessons learned" you want, but if you don't implement changes to procedures, you're simply wasting time and money.

Successful Hyperscale Data Centers

TO PROVIDE CONTEXT and insight into what makes a hyperscale data center project successful, we will examine case studies from various industries, including technology, finance, e-commerce, healthcare, and government. These case studies illustrate the challenges faced, the solutions implemented, and the outcomes achieved.

Case Study 1: Tech Industry Giant

OVERVIEW: This case study focuses on a leading technology company that built a hyperscale data center to support its global cloud services. Located in a region with abundant renewable energy resources, the facility allows the company to power its operations sustainably.

Challenges:

- Securing land in a densely populated area.
- Managing environmental concerns related to water usage.
- Meeting aggressive timelines to stay ahead of demand.

Solutions:

- **Modular Design:** Implemented a modular design that allowed for rapid expansion as demand increased, reducing construction time and costs by 20%.
- **Power Purchase Agreement (PPA):** Negotiated a PPA with a local renewable energy provider, securing 80% of the facility's energy needs from wind and solar sources.
- **Advanced Cooling Technologies:** Deployed liquid immersion cooling systems, reducing water consumption by 70% compared to traditional methods.

Lessons Learned:

- **Flexibility:** The modular design allowed for quick scalability and adaptation to changing market conditions.
- **Environmental Considerations:** Addressing environmental concerns early in the project helped avoid regulatory delays and fostered community support.
- **Strategic Location:** Choosing a location with access to renewable energy and a strong fiber backbone was crucial for long-term sustainability and connectivity.

Case Study 2: Financial Sector Leader

OVERVIEW: A major financial institution built a hyperscale data center to support its high-frequency trading operations. The data center is strategically located near a financial hub to minimize latency and maximize transaction speeds.

Challenges:

- Meeting stringent security requirements to protect sensitive financial data.
- Managing the high power demands of the facility.

Solutions:

- **Robust Security Measures:** Implemented state-of-the-art physical and cyber security systems, including multi-factor authentication, biometric access controls, and real-time threat detection.
- **Power Redundancy:** Established a partnership with local utility providers to create a dual-feed power supply, ensuring 99.999% uptime.

Lessons Learned:

- **Security:** Robust security measures are non-negotiable for protecting financial data and maintaining trust with clients.
- **Proximity to Financial Hubs:** Locating the data center near a financial hub minimized latency, which is critical in high-frequency trading.
- **Power Redundancy:** A reliable, redundant power supply

is essential for preventing outages that could cost millions in lost transactions.

Case Study 3: E-Commerce Powerhouse

OVERVIEW: A leading e-commerce company built a hyperscale data center to handle the massive influx of online orders and customer data during peak shopping seasons.

Challenges:

- Managing scalability during high-traffic periods like Black Friday and Cyber Monday.
- Ensuring robust cybersecurity amid heightened threats.

Solutions:

- **Scalable Architecture:** Utilized a cloud-native, container-based architecture to dynamically allocate resources based on real-time demand.
- **Advanced Cybersecurity Measures:** Deployed AI-driven cybersecurity solutions, including anomaly detection and automated response systems, reducing incident response times by 50%.

Lessons Learned:

- **Scalability:** Dynamic, scalable architecture was key to handling traffic spikes without performance degradation.
- **Cybersecurity:** Proactive and adaptive cybersecurity measures were necessary to protect against evolving

threats.

- **Customer Experience:** Ensuring the data center could handle high volumes without compromising performance was critical for customer satisfaction and retention.

Case Study 4: Healthcare Data Center

OVERVIEW: A major healthcare provider built a hyperscale data center to manage vast amounts of patient data and support telemedicine services, adhering to stringent regulations around data security and patient privacy.

CHALLENGES:

- Ensuring HIPAA compliance and securing patient data.
- Maintaining uptime during critical operations like surgeries and patient monitoring.

Solutions:

- **HIPAA-Compliant Architecture:** Designed the data center with multi-layered encryption, access controls, and audit trails.
- **Telemedicine Integration:** Implemented low-latency infrastructure to support real-time telemedicine services.
- **Resilient Power Systems:** Installed redundant power supplies and backup generators with a failover time of less than one second.

Lessons Learned:

- **Regulatory Compliance:** Close collaboration with legal and compliance teams ensured adherence to healthcare regulations.
- **Continuous Availability:** Redundant systems were essential for maintaining uptime during critical healthcare operations.
- **Data Security:** Advanced encryption and monitoring systems protected sensitive patient data against breaches.

Case Study 5: Government Data Center

OVERVIEW: A government agency built a hyperscale data center for managing national security data and public service applications, requiring the highest levels of security and redundancy.

Challenges:

- Meeting national security protocols and integrating with legacy systems.
- Ensuring geographic redundancy to protect against regional disasters.

Solutions:

- **National Security Protocols:** Implemented military-grade security, including continuous surveillance and multi-factor authentication.
- **Legacy System Integration:** Developed a phased integration plan for legacy systems, ensuring minimal

disruption.

- **Geographic Redundancy:** Established a secondary data center at a geographically distant location to provide failover capabilities.

Lessons Learned:

- **Security First:** Uncompromising security measures were necessary to protect sensitive government data.
- **Integration Challenges:** Careful planning and phased implementation were required to integrate with legacy systems.
- **Disaster Recovery:** Geographic redundancy was crucial for maintaining operational continuity during regional disruptions.

Lessons from Failures

WHILE THE ABOVE CASE studies highlight successes, it's equally important to learn from projects that faced setbacks or failures. Understanding what went wrong can provide valuable insights to help prevent similar issues in future projects.

What Went Wrong:

- **Underestimated Complexity:** Some projects failed to account for the complexity of integrating new technology with legacy systems, leading to delays and cost overruns.
- **Insufficient Planning:** Inadequate planning around

power redundancy and cooling systems caused significant operational issues once the data center went live.

- **Vendor Failures:** Poor vendor management and lack of proper vetting led to critical components being delayed or failing to meet specifications.

Recovery Efforts:

- **Revised Strategies:** Projects were salvaged by adopting phased implementations or bringing in expert consultants to re-evaluate plans.
- **Improved Documentation:** Enhanced documentation and communication protocols were established to prevent similar mistakes.
- **Stronger Contracts:** Future projects incorporated stronger contractual terms, including penalties for non-performance and tighter controls.

Innovation and Collaboration

Role of Innovation:

- **Cutting-Edge Technologies:** Successful projects utilized AI-driven monitoring systems, such as predictive analytics for preventive maintenance, and advanced cooling techniques like liquid immersion cooling to enhance efficiency and reduce costs.
- **Process Innovations:** Employed novel approaches like modular builds and just-in-time delivery systems to

streamline construction, minimize disruptions, and reduce overall project timelines by 30%.

Collaboration and Teamwork:

- **Team Dynamics:** Effective communication and collaboration were vital across different project phases, enabling teams to identify and address challenges quickly.
- **Conflict Resolution:** Proactively resolving conflicts through regular stakeholder meetings and workshops helped keep projects on track.

Post-Implementation Impact

Performance Metrics:

- **Uptime and Reliability:** Most data centers exceeded expectations in terms of uptime and reliability, achieving 99.999% uptime due to robust redundancy systems.
- **Energy Efficiency:** Advanced energy management practices, such as dynamic cooling adjustments and renewable energy integration, led to a 25% reduction in operational costs.

Client Feedback:

- **High Satisfaction:** Clients reported high levels of satisfaction with the flexibility and scalability of the data centers.

- **Areas for Improvement:** Feedback highlighted the need for better initial planning around future scalability and technology upgrades.

Best Practices and Recommendations

- **Document Everything:** Comprehensive documentation is critical for tracking progress, identifying issues, and making informed decisions. Ensure that lessons learned are translated into actionable changes.
- **Prioritize Security and Compliance:** Invest in top-tier security technologies and maintain rigorous compliance with industry regulations to mitigate risks.
- **Plan for Scalability:** Design data centers with scalability in mind to accommodate both seasonal spikes and long-term growth.
- **Engage Stakeholders Early:** Early engagement with stakeholders, including local authorities, helps prevent delays and builds community support.
- **Invest in Redundancy:** Ensure redundant systems for power, cooling, and networking to maintain uptime and resilience.
- **Learn from Failures:** Analyze and document failures as thoroughly as successes to avoid repeating mistakes.

WORKING IN THE MISSION-critical space teaches that despite the best-laid plans, challenges will arise. Projects may face unexpected issues, and even meticulous documentation can't prevent every problem. However, by learning from past experiences, documenting everything thoroughly, and remaining flexible, you can navigate these challenges successfully. These case studies provide valuable insights and lessons that can guide future projects, helping to build data centers that are not only successful but also resilient and adaptable to changing conditions.

The Future of Hyperscale Data Centers

AS WE NEAR THE CONCLUSION of our journey through the intricate world of hyperscale data centers, it's evident that the industry stands at a pivotal moment. Rapid technological advancements, evolving regulatory landscapes, and shifting market demands are reshaping how these facilities are designed, constructed, and managed. The hyperscale data centers of the future will be defined by their ability to embrace and leverage new technologies that drive efficiency, sustainability, and reliability. This chapter explores these emerging trends and innovations, drawing lessons from past technological cycles to anticipate the future and examining the broader implications of these changes, including regulatory challenges, economic considerations, and the need for a skilled workforce.

Future Trends in Hyperscale Data Centers

THE DATA CENTERS OF tomorrow will be characterized by their adaptability, scalability, and innovative use of cutting-edge technologies. Here are some of the key trends shaping the future of hyperscale data centers:

1. AI and Machine Learning: Revolutionizing Operations

- **AI-Driven Automation:**
  Artificial Intelligence (AI) is poised to revolutionize data center operations by automating tasks, from monitoring and diagnostics to predictive maintenance and energy management. For example, AI-driven systems can optimize cooling processes in real-time, significantly reducing energy consumption. Google's use of DeepMind AI to manage its data center cooling systems has resulted in a 40% reduction in cooling energy. AI will be integral in achieving greater efficiency, reducing human error, and minimizing downtime.
- **Predictive Analytics:**
  Machine learning algorithms will enable predictive analytics, allowing data centers to foresee potential equipment failures, performance bottlenecks, or security breaches before they occur. By analyzing historical and real-time data, these algorithms help data centers transition from a reactive to a proactive maintenance model, reducing costs and extending the lifespan of critical infrastructure.

2. Advanced Cooling Techniques

- **Immersion Cooling:**
  As data centers become denser and computing power increases, traditional air-cooling methods may no longer

suffice. Immersion cooling, where servers are submerged in a thermally conductive liquid, offers superior heat dissipation and energy efficiency. This technique eliminates the need for fans and air conditioning, significantly lowering energy costs. Companies like Microsoft have deployed two-phase immersion cooling in their Azure data centers, achieving better thermal efficiency and reduced operational costs. This method will play a crucial role in maintaining performance without compromising energy efficiency as workloads become more demanding.

- **Two-Phase Immersion Cooling:**
  Involves immersing servers in a specialized dielectric fluid that boils off at low temperatures, absorbing heat directly from the components. The vapor then condenses back into a liquid, creating a continuous cooling cycle. This method allows for even higher server densities and reduced energy consumption, making it ideal for high-computing power applications such as AI model training and high-frequency trading.

3. Energy Innovation and Sustainability

- **Shift to Lithium-Ion Batteries:**
  Lithium-ion batteries are being adopted in data centers for their higher energy density, longer lifespan, and reduced environmental impact compared to traditional lead-acid batteries. AWS has transitioned to lithium-ion

solutions in its data centers, benefiting from faster recharge times and better energy efficiency. This shift aligns with the broader trend toward sustainable energy solutions and offers substantial savings in operational costs and carbon footprint.

- **Jet Turbine Power Generation:**
  Jet turbines are emerging as a viable power solution for data centers, especially in mission-critical environments where uptime is paramount. These turbines can quickly generate large amounts of power and offer flexibility by running on multiple fuel sources, including natural gas and biofuels. While they require significant initial investment, their reliability, efficiency, and lower maintenance costs make them attractive for facilities where continuous power supply is critical.
- **Renewable Energy Integration:**
  Integrating on-site renewable energy sources such as solar and wind power, along with advanced energy storage systems, is becoming a priority for data centers aiming to reduce their carbon footprint. Facebook's data center in Oregon, for example, uses a combination of solar energy and battery storage to maintain a steady power supply while minimizing environmental impact. As environmental regulations become stricter, these renewable strategies will enhance sustainability and provide a competitive edge.

4. Edge Computing and Micro Data Centers

- **Proliferation of Edge Data Centers:**
  The growth of edge computing is driven by the need for low-latency data processing and real-time analytics for applications such as autonomous vehicles, augmented reality, and remote surgery. Companies like Equinix and Digital Realty are investing heavily in edge infrastructure to support these use cases. By processing data closer to the end-user, edge data centers reduce latency, lower bandwidth costs, and improve service quality. This trend will accelerate, complementing traditional hyperscale data centers by distributing computing resources closer to where data is generated and consumed.
- **Micro Data Centers:**
  Compact, self-contained units provide localized computing resources in remote or underserved areas, offering flexibility and scalability. These units can be deployed quickly and customized to meet specific needs, making them ideal for supporting edge computing and IoT applications. As the demand for real-time processing grows, micro data centers will expand data center capabilities beyond traditional boundaries.

5. Modular and Containerized Data Centers

- **Prefabricated Modular Data Centers:**
  Prefabricated, modular data centers are becoming

popular due to their ability to be quickly deployed and scaled to meet demand. This modular approach allows for more efficient use of capital and faster deployment times. For example, Alibaba has adopted a modular approach, enabling rapid scaling while minimizing initial capital expenditures. This flexibility is advantageous in markets with rapidly changing demand or regulatory environments.

- **Containerized Data Centers:**
  Housing data centers in shipping containers offers significant flexibility and mobility, making them ideal for rapid deployment in diverse environments, from urban centers to remote locations. These data centers can be pre-assembled and tested off-site, reducing construction time and costs. They are useful in scenarios requiring temporary or emergency computing resources, such as disaster recovery operations or high-capacity computing events.

6. Quantum Computing Readiness

- **Quantum-Safe Cryptography:**
  As quantum computing moves closer to reality, data centers must prepare by adopting quantum-safe encryption methods to protect sensitive data. Traditional encryption algorithms could become obsolete with the advent of quantum computers, which can break them much faster than classical computers. Ensuring data

centers are ready for this shift is critical to maintaining security and compliance.

- **Hybrid Quantum-Classical Computing:**
  While quantum computing is still in its infancy, data centers must plan for its integration alongside traditional computing infrastructure. This hybrid model allows data centers to leverage quantum computing's unique capabilities, such as solving complex optimization problems or simulating molecular structures, while still using classical computing for routine tasks. As quantum technology matures, seamless integration of these systems will be a competitive differentiator.

7. 5G and Network Innovation

- **Low-Latency Applications:**
  The rollout of 5G networks will drive demand for data centers supporting applications requiring ultra-low latency, such as augmented reality, autonomous driving, and smart cities. Strategic location planning and enhanced networking infrastructure will be essential to meet these demands, particularly in sectors like finance and healthcare, where milliseconds matter.
- **Network Slicing:**
  Data centers will need to handle 5G network slicing, which allows multiple virtual networks to operate on a single physical network. This capability will enable more efficient use of network resources and provide tailored

services for different applications, from high-priority emergency services to standard consumer traffic.

8. Enhanced Security and Compliance

- **Zero Trust Architecture:**
  As cyber threats evolve, data centers will increasingly adopt a zero-trust security model that requires continuous verification of every access request, both internal and external. This approach assumes threats could come from anywhere and emphasizes strict access controls, constant monitoring, and granular segmentation of networks to minimize breach impact.
- **Biometric Access Controls:**
  Biometric technologies, such as fingerprint scanners, facial recognition, and retina scans, will become standard for physical security in data centers. These advanced systems provide an additional layer of protection against unauthorized access, ensuring that only vetted and authorized personnel can access sensitive areas.

9. Software-Defined Everything (SDx)

- **Software-Defined Networking (SDN):**
  SDN will enable more flexible and efficient network management, reducing costs and improving agility. By separating the control plane from the data plane, SDN allows network administrators to programmatically control traffic flow, optimize network resources, and

respond quickly to changing demands.

- **Software-Defined Data Centers (SDDC):**
  The virtualization of the entire data center infrastructure, from compute and storage to networking, will provide greater scalability and operational efficiency. SDDC enables data centers to be managed entirely through software, allowing for more agile deployment, faster upgrades, and easier integration with public and private clouds.

10. Automation and Robotics

- **Robotic Process Automation (RPA):**
  Robots will increasingly be used in data centers for tasks like monitoring systems, performing physical maintenance, and moving equipment. This trend enhances operational efficiency, reduces the risk of human error, and improves safety by minimizing human involvement in potentially hazardous activities.
- **Drones for Inspections:**
  Drones equipped with cameras and sensors will be deployed for regular inspections, particularly in hard-to-reach areas such as rooftops or high-security zones. Drones offer a faster, safer, and more cost-effective way to conduct routine inspections, detect issues early, and reduce downtime.

11. High-Density Storage Solutions

- **DNA Data Storage:**
  Emerging technologies like DNA data storage, which encodes data in the form of DNA sequences, could revolutionize data storage. This method offers unprecedented density, durability, and stability, potentially storing exabytes of data in a space no larger than a sugar cube. While still in its experimental stages, DNA storage holds immense promise for the future.
- **Holographic Storage:**
  Holographic storage, which uses three-dimensional recording to store data, offers a significant increase in capacity without requiring additional physical space. This technology could be vital for future high-capacity storage needs, enabling data centers to handle growing volumes of information more efficiently.

12. Renewable and Sustainable Practices

- **Waterless Cooling Solutions:**
  New cooling technologies that minimize or eliminate water use will reduce the environmental impact of data centers, particularly in regions where water is scarce. Innovations such as dry cooling, which uses air instead of water, and liquid cooling, which reduces the need for water-based chillers, are gaining traction in the industry.
- **Carbon Capture and Utilization:**

Data centers will increasingly explore carbon capture technologies to reduce emissions and contribute to sustainability goals. Carbon capture can involve capturing CO_2 emissions from power generation and other processes, then storing it underground or converting it into useful products. These practices will become increasingly important as regulatory pressure mounts to reduce greenhouse gas emissions.

13. Blockchain and Decentralized Data Centers (Cryptocurrency/Bitcoin)

- **Decentralized Data Centers:**
  Blockchain technology could enable the creation of decentralized data centers that enhance security and resilience by distributing data across multiple locations. This approach leverages the distributed ledger model to create a network of interconnected data centers, providing greater redundancy and making it harder for a single point of failure to disrupt operations.

14. Regulatory and Compliance Challenges

- **Global Regulations:**
  As data centers expand globally, they must navigate a complex web of regulations that vary by region. These include data sovereignty laws, environmental regulations, and labor laws. Understanding and complying with these regulations is critical to avoiding legal penalties and ensuring smooth operations.

- **GDPR and Data Protection:**
  With the increasing amount of sensitive data handled by data centers, compliance with data protection regulations like GDPR and CCPA is more important than ever. Data centers must implement robust measures to ensure that data is stored and processed in accordance with these stringent requirements.

15. Economic and Market Considerations

- **Cost Management:**
  The adoption of new technologies and the demand for greater efficiency are driving up the costs of building and maintaining hyperscale data centers. Strategies for managing these costs, such as modular construction and energy-efficient designs, will be essential for maintaining profitability.
- **Market Trends:**
  Understanding market trends, such as the shift towards green data centers or the growing demand for edge computing, is crucial for staying competitive. Data centers that can adapt to these trends will be better positioned to succeed in the long term.

16. Disaster Recovery and Business Continuity Planning

- **Resilience Against Natural Disasters:**
  Climate change is increasing the frequency and severity of extreme weather events. Data centers must be designed

to withstand these events and have robust disaster recovery plans in place to ensure business continuity.

- **Business Continuity Plans (BCP):**
  Having a comprehensive BCP is essential for ensuring that operations can continue or quickly resume after a disruption. This includes backup power systems, data redundancy, and emergency response protocols.

17. Human Capital and Talent Management

- **Skilled Workforce:**
  As technology evolves, so too does the need for a skilled workforce. Recruiting and retaining talent with expertise in AI, cybersecurity, and advanced data center operations will be a major challenge for the industry.
- **Training and Development:**
  Ongoing training and upskilling are essential for keeping staff current with the latest technologies and best practices. Investing in employee development improves performance and helps retain top talent.

18. Customer Experience and Service Delivery

- **Customer-Centric Approaches:**
  As data centers increasingly serve diverse industries, offering tailored services to meet specific customer needs will be key. This includes providing customization options and maintaining high service levels through well-defined SLAs.

- **Hybrid Cloud Solutions:**
  The rise of hybrid cloud environments means data centers must offer seamless integration with public and private clouds. Flexibility in service offerings will be crucial to meeting customer expectations.

Justin's Thoughts

THE FUTURE OF HYPERSCALE data centers is bright, filled with opportunities to leverage emerging technologies and drive the industry forward. However, success in this rapidly evolving field requires more than just adopting the latest innovations. It demands a commitment to adaptability, continuous improvement, and a forward-thinking approach that anticipates the challenges of tomorrow.

Adaptability and Innovation

- **Learning from the Past:**
  Just as we saw during the dot-com era, technology evolves in cycles—becoming smaller, faster, and more efficient. Today's data centers must be prepared to adapt to these changes to remain relevant and competitive.
- **Embrace the Future:**
  Whether it's integrating AI, shifting to more sustainable energy sources, or preparing for the quantum computing revolution, embracing new technologies and being willing to innovate are critical for long-term success in the data center industry.

THE INDUSTRY IS AT a pivotal moment, driven by rapid advancements in technology and increasing demands for efficiency, sustainability, and reliability.

The decisions you make in designing, building, and operating these facilities have far-reaching consequences, not just for your business but for the world at large. Treating this endeavor as the serious business it is—one that requires both strategic thinking and meticulous attention to detail—will ensure that your data center is not just a functional building but a critical asset that drives value and innovation for years to come.

Remember, in this fast-paced, ever-evolving field, the mission is truly critical. Approach it with the seriousness it deserves, and you will not only succeed but thrive in this vital industry.

Chapter 11: Bringing It All Together

AS WE COME TO THE END of this book, it's time to step back and look at the bigger picture: the practical, no-nonsense approach to building and operating a hyperscale data center. We've gone through the details – from site selection, design, and engineering to financial planning, vendor management, and commissioning. We've examined case studies and future trends. Now, it's time to distill everything down into plain, straightforward terms.

The Mission is Critical, But It's Not Complicated

Let's be clear: building and running a data center is a significant undertaking, but it doesn't have to be as complicated as it often seems. Sure, the industry throws around terms like "hyperscale," "edge computing," and "quantum readiness," and yes, there are complex technologies involved. But at its core, building a data center is like any other business endeavor. It boils down to a few fundamental principles: know your numbers, manage your risks, and keep things simple.

A Quick, No-Nonsense Rundown

HERE'S THE DEAL: A data center is just a massive, secure building filled with equipment that needs to stay cool, powered, and connected 24/7. That's it. Everything else – the tech jargon, the marketing hype, the latest buzzwords – can distract you from these basics. The key to success is to approach data center development like any other construction project, with a clear focus on your business objectives.

1. **Know Your Purpose and Stick to It**
   Before you start, be clear on the purpose of your data

center. Is it to support cloud computing? AI workloads? High-frequency trading? Each purpose will dictate specific design and operational needs. Don't try to be everything to everyone. Know what your center needs to accomplish, and focus on that.

2. **Location is Key – But Don't Overthink It**
   Choose a site that meets your basic needs: enough space, access to power, good connectivity, and minimal risk from natural disasters. Don't waste time finding the "perfect" site; find one that works, negotiate a fair price, and move forward. Remember, data centers are business decisions – not passion projects. If repurposing an old building makes more sense than building from scratch, do it.
3. **Design Smart, Not Fancy**
   When it comes to design, prioritize simplicity and scalability. Stick to tried-and-true designs that can be adapted to your needs. Focus on the essentials: efficient cooling, reliable power, and robust security. Don't get distracted by flashy features that add cost but no real value. The goal is to create a space that is flexible, functional, and easy to manage.
4. **Manage Your Costs Like a Hawk**
   Every decision in the data center construction process should tie back to one simple question: How does this affect the bottom line? Whether it's choosing between a modular or traditional build, negotiating with vendors, or selecting cooling technologies – every decision should make financial sense. Avoid overspending on unproven technologies or proprietary solutions that lock you into a

specific vendor. Focus on scalability, energy efficiency, and cost control.

5. **Prioritize Redundancy Where It Matters**
When it comes to redundancy, focus on what's critical. You don't need to gold-plate every system, but you must ensure that your core infrastructure – power, cooling, and network – has sufficient backup. Use the 2N redundancy model where zero downtime is essential, like in financial transactions or healthcare. For less critical functions, an N+1 or N+2 model might suffice. The point is to balance cost with reliability – you want to be covered but not overextended.
6. **Document, Document, Document**
From planning to commissioning, document everything. Proper documentation isn't just a best practice; it's essential for continuity, compliance, and ongoing operations. It helps track changes, identify issues, and implement lessons learned. This step isn't glamorous, but it's crucial. You don't want to rely on someone's memory or best guess when things go wrong.
7. **Build Relationships and Leverage Expertise**
Don't try to reinvent the wheel. Partner with vendors, consultants, and contractors who have experience in data center projects. Maintain good relationships with local authorities and community leaders. Engage with the community early and often – this helps smooth over potential conflicts and build local support. Remember, collaboration is key.
8. **Commission and Test Like You Mean It**
Before going live, test everything thoroughly. Every

component should be tested under load, and every failover mechanism should be tried in real-life scenarios. Don't assume anything will work just because it looks good on paper. Invest in robust commissioning and testing processes to catch issues early.

9. **Keep Operations Lean and Focused on Uptime**
   Once operational, the goal is simple: Keep the data center running smoothly with minimal downtime. Use automation, AI, and monitoring systems to identify and solve problems before they impact service. Prioritize maintenance and invest in ongoing training for your team. Remember, uptime is king – everything else supports this primary objective.
10. **Adapt and Innovate as You Grow**
   The data center industry is constantly evolving. Stay flexible and ready to adapt. Embrace new technologies like AI, edge computing, and renewable energy, but only if they make financial and operational sense. Don't chase trends – focus on innovations that align with your business goals.

Back to Basics: It's All About the Numbers

AT THE END OF THE DAY, building a data center boils down to numbers: size, capacity, power, redundancy, uptime, and cost. You must know your numbers and ensure they align with your business objectives. Everything else is secondary. You're not building a monument; you're building a critical piece of infrastructure that needs to operate efficiently and profitably.

Let's Break It Down Simply:

1. **Size and Capacity:**
   Determine how big your data center needs to be and what it will hold. Plan for growth, but don't overbuild. Space costs money – make sure every square foot is justified.
2. **Power:**
   How much power do you need, and where will it come from? Secure a reliable power supply and consider redundancy options. Think about future scalability – can you increase power without massive costs?
3. **Redundancy:**
   Decide where you need redundancy and to what extent. It's all about balancing cost with reliability. Too little redundancy, and you risk downtime; too much, and you waste resources.
4. **Uptime:**
   This is your primary metric for success. Everything revolves around maintaining high uptime. Invest in monitoring, predictive maintenance, and robust testing to achieve this.
5. **Cost:**
   From construction to operation, always be clear on costs. Know where every dollar is going and why. Track expenses closely and avoid unnecessary expenditures. Remember, every cost must tie back to your core objectives – reliability, efficiency, and growth.

A Practical, No-Drama Approach

DON'T LET THE COMPLEXITY of the data center industry fool you into overcomplicating your approach. Yes, there are many moving parts, but at its heart, a data center is just another business venture. It requires planning, execution, and management – the same basic principles that apply to any business.

Forget the hype and focus on the fundamentals. Do your homework, know your numbers, and approach every decision with clarity and purpose. Keep it simple, straightforward, and aligned with your core business goals.

Lessons from Other Industries: Keeping It Simple Works

THINK ABOUT INDUSTRIES that have thrived by sticking to basics. Successful retailers focus on inventory turnover and customer experience. Manufacturing giants optimize production efficiency and supply chain management. Airlines focus on load factors, fuel efficiency, and route optimization. In every case, the key to success has been a laser focus on the numbers that matter, with an eye on cost control and profitability.

Building and operating a data center is no different. It requires the same disciplined approach to managing costs, optimizing performance, and delivering value. Don't let the technology intimidate you – keep your eyes on the prize and remember that it all comes down to numbers.

The Power of Simplicity: Why Overcomplicating Hurts You

OVERCOMPLICATING THE process doesn't just waste time – it costs money. Each additional layer of complexity adds potential points of failure and increases operational costs. Unnecessary bells and whistles can delay your timeline, blow your budget, and distract your team from the real goal – building a data center that works efficiently and effectively.

Ask yourself: Are you adding features or processes because they add real value or because they sound impressive? Every decision should have a clear, quantifiable benefit. If it doesn't, skip it. Complexity for its own sake is your enemy.

Treat It Like a Business

THE MOST IMPORTANT takeaway from this book is that building and operating a data center should be treated like any other business decision. It's about being strategic, managing risks, and staying focused on your core objectives. You don't need to be a tech guru or a construction expert to succeed – you need to be a smart, disciplined manager who understands the value of keeping things simple.

- **Plan Carefully** – Understand your objectives, choose a suitable location, design a smart facility, and control costs.
- **Execute Meticulously** – Stick to proven methods, manage your vendors, and test everything thoroughly.
- **Operate Efficiently** – Focus on uptime, keep your operations lean, and adapt as needed.
- **Adapt Continually** – Stay informed about industry trends, embrace change when it adds value, and always look for ways to improve.

The Bottom Line: Keep It Simple, Keep It Smart

REMEMBER, THIS IS A business like any other. Your goal is to create a functional, reliable, and profitable data center. Stick to the basics, stay focused on the numbers, and make decisions that align with your core objectives. When you strip away the jargon, the buzzwords, and the hype, it all comes down to this: a data center is just another business – treat it as such, and you will succeed.

The mission is indeed critical, but it doesn't have to be complicated. Focus on what matters most, keep things straightforward, and you'll find that building and running a data center is not only manageable but a rewarding venture that drives value and growth for years to come.

Chapter 12: Business Models and Strategic Considerations for Hyperscale Data Centers

OWNING A HYPERSCALE data center presents a unique set of opportunities and challenges. The hyperscale space can be lucrative, but like any business, it comes with risks, particularly in a rapidly evolving industry. The key to success lies in adopting a business model that minimizes active management, avoids heavy investments in rapidly depreciating technology, and leverages passive income streams. This chapter explores various business models and strategies for maximizing profitability while maintaining flexibility and minimizing risks.

Emphasizing a Passive Income Model

THE ULTIMATE GOAL FOR many data center owners is to establish a business that operates with minimal active involvement, generating passive income through strategic leasing and infrastructure management. To achieve this, the focus should be on creating a robust infrastructure that can attract long-term tenants without the owner needing to manage the day-to-day operations or invest heavily in specific technologies.

1. Infrastructure Leasing: The Landlord Model

FOCUS ON LEASING SPACE, Power, and Cooling: By adopting a landlord model, data center owners can lease essential infrastructure—such as space, power, and cooling capabilities—without getting involved in the technology that runs within the facility. This approach simplifies operations, reduces the need for specialized expertise, and avoids the financial risks associated with technology obsolescence.

Triple Net Leases (NNN): Implementing triple net leases (NNN) shifts the responsibility for property taxes, insurance, and maintenance costs to the tenants. This lease structure significantly reduces the owner's operational burdens and ensures a steady, predictable income stream with minimal overhead.

Avoiding Technology Investments: Instead of purchasing servers, networking equipment, or other IT assets, focus solely on providing a scalable infrastructure. Tenants bring their own technology, allowing them to customize their setup according to their needs while the owner provides a reliable environment. This strategy reduces the financial risk tied to technology depreciation and shifts the responsibility for technology management to the tenants.

2. Power Sales: Proceed with Caution

SELLING POWER AS A Service: Selling power directly to tenants or back to the grid can be a potential revenue stream. However, this requires navigating complex regulatory landscapes and can introduce additional liabilities. While it may be profitable, it's essential to understand the legal requirements and market conditions fully. Consulting with legal and energy experts is critical to avoid pitfalls.

Keep Power Sales Simple: If pursuing power sales, keep the arrangements straightforward. Avoid long-term power purchase commitments that could expose the business to fluctuating energy prices or regulatory changes. Simpler, flexible agreements that allow for periodic adjustments can help mitigate these risks.

3. Connectivity and Colocation Services

COLOCATION SPACE LEASING: Providing colocation services allows tenants to rent space within the facility to house their own servers and equipment. This service requires minimal technological input from the owner, as tenants manage their hardware and IT needs. The owner's role remains largely passive, focusing on maintaining the facility and ensuring reliable power and cooling.

Offering Cross-Connects and Meet-Me Rooms: Enhancing the facility with connectivity options such as cross-connects and meet-me rooms can add value without requiring significant technology investments. Tenants pay for the connectivity rights, which can be a lucrative addition to the leasing revenue.

4. Leveraging Long-Term Leases

SECURING LONG-TERM Tenants: Focus on long-term leases with reliable tenants to ensure a steady cash flow and reduce risks associated with frequent tenant turnover. Long-term leases simplify financial forecasting and provide stability in the business model.

Maximizing NNN Leases: By locking in NNN leases, most operational and financial responsibilities are transferred to the tenants, further reducing the owner's need for active involvement and making the data center a more passive investment.

5. Utilizing Tax Incentives and Strategic Financing

EXPLOITING TAX INCENTIVES: Take advantage of tax incentives available for data centers, such as accelerated depreciation, renewable energy credits, or local grants. These can significantly reduce costs and enhance profitability, especially when aligned with infrastructure investments like energy-efficient upgrades.

Financing with Minimal Equity: Consider financing models that require minimal equity input from the owner. Options like Real Estate Investment Trusts (REITs) can spread financial risk and attract institutional investors looking for passive income. This approach helps mitigate the capital burden and enhances the data center's appeal as a low-risk, high-reward asset.

6. Future-Proofing with Minimal Investment

SCALABLE, MODULAR INFRASTRUCTURE: Invest in scalable, modular infrastructure that can be easily expanded or upgraded without significant disruption. This approach allows the data center to grow with demand while minimizing upfront costs. Modular solutions also make the facility adaptable to a variety of tenant needs, increasing marketability.

Strategic Environmental Certifications: While certifications such as LEED or WELL can add value, it's crucial to evaluate their relevance to your target tenant base. For example, cryptocurrency miners may not value green certifications, whereas tech firms focused on AI or machine learning may see them as essential. Opt for certifications that offer the best return on investment and align with the facility's operational model.

7. Generating Revenue through Additional Services

OFFERING ENHANCED SERVICES at a Premium: While the primary model focuses on basic leasing, consider offering additional services at a premium. These can include enhanced security options, dedicated bandwidth, or premium cooling services. By keeping these as optional add-ons, the core business remains passive while still allowing for revenue growth through value-added services.

Flexible Contract Terms: Offering flexible contract terms that allow tenants to scale their services up or down can be appealing. This flexibility can attract a broader range of tenants and accommodate those with variable needs, such as startups or seasonal businesses.

8. Navigating Market Volatility: Lessons from the Dot-Com Era

CAUTION IN OVEREXPANSION: The hyperscale space, like any market, can be cyclical. The dot-com era taught us that rapid expansion without securing long-term revenue can lead to financial instability. Proceed with caution, and avoid overbuilding in anticipation of demand that may not materialize.

Locking in Clients: Focus on locking clients into long-term leases, particularly with NNN terms, to ensure ongoing revenue even if the market cools. These agreements provide financial security and allow for better management of cash flow during periods of market uncertainty.

Avoiding Technology Overhead: One of the key lessons is to avoid becoming too entangled with specific technologies. By focusing on infrastructure and leasing, the business remains insulated from rapid technological changes that can render equipment obsolete. This approach not only mitigates risk but also aligns the data center's financial model with its long-term, passive investment strategy.

Keeping It Simple and Profitable

THE BUSINESS MODEL for owning a hyperscale data center should revolve around simplicity, stability, and risk management. By avoiding heavy investments in technology and focusing on leasing and infrastructure, you can build a profitable, largely passive income stream. Use caution in market speculation, leverage long-term leases, and maximize tax benefits and incentives to enhance your financial returns.

Always remember, the goal is to do as little as possible on the operational front while maximizing revenue through smart leasing strategies and minimal capital expenditure. The hyperscale space offers significant opportunities, but the key to success lies in a disciplined, strategic approach that emphasizes infrastructure over technology and focuses on long-term, passive income.

The End

Dear Reader,

Thanks for sticking with me through this journey into hyperscale data centers. I hope you found the insights valuable and picked up a few strategies that can help you tackle your own projects data center or not.

Remember, at the core of it all what it all boils down to, it's about clear planning, smart decisions, and not overcomplicating things. Whether you're building a data center or running any other business, the principles remain the same: keep your eyes on the numbers, stay flexible, and always plan ahead.

If you have any questions or want to dive deeper into anything we covered or anything construction related, just look me up on LinkedIn—I'm always happy to chat. Thanks again for reading, and best of luck with your ventures!

Justin DeFillippo

P.S. Remember the "hype" in Hyperscale is just that.. It's just a data center. Just a big box with power, cooling and internet access... Don't overthink it.

Special Thanks

Acknowledgments

Over the years, so many of you have helped shape who I am today. Whether through friendship, guidance, mentorship, or simply by being a part of my journey even if it was just a moment in time, each of you has left an impact on my life, and for that, I am truly grateful.

Special Thanks To: (Not in order of importance lol)

First and foremost, I want to thank God for guiding me through the many ups and downs of life. Every high and low was necessary, for without the good times and the challenges, this book—and the incredible people I've met along the way—would not exist.

To my incredible wife and best friend, Sandra DeFillippo, thank you for your unwavering support, love, and encouragement. You are my rock.

To my mom Reena DeFillippo, dad Michael DeFillippo, sister Jennifer DeFillippo, and my entire family, your support has meant the world to me.

Brian Yurkins, Christine DeFillippo, David Dolman, Harry Morales, Robert Berentsen, Luis Lopez, Jia Wei Chen, David Lavender, John Hilt, Terry Sherman, Louis Dellavalle Jr, Dennis Saleeby, Brian Orr, Anthony Gironta, Michael Brown, Richard Martucci, Dan Ryan, Rafik Mishreki, David Wechsler, Mario Klimczuk, Thomas Amodio, Harry Shasho, Christopher Keddy, Anthony Focca, Nic DeGirolamo, Robert Eccles, Fernando Quijano Jr, Kevin Adams, Noel Kane, Jose Cambrelen, Jennifer Cardella Appice, Lenny Censi, Mark Comerford, Tomka Madison, Anthony DeMeo, Patrick Dempsey, and Carol Romeo.

Each of you has made a lasting impact on my life, and for that, I am deeply grateful. I wish nothing but the best for each of you, and I hope our paths continue to cross. Thank you for being a part of my journey.

In Loving Memory Of:

Frank Farrugia and Peter Romeo— thank you for everything.

Glossary

A&E (ARCHITECTURE AND Engineering): Disciplines involved in the design and engineering of construction projects, including data centers.

AC (Alternating Current): A type of electrical current in which the direction of flow reverses periodically, commonly used in power distribution.

ACM (Asbestos-Containing Material): Any material or product that contains more than 1% asbestos. In construction, ACMs are significant due to the health hazards associated with asbestos exposure. Proper handling, abatement, and disposal of ACMs are critical to comply with safety regulations and prevent asbestos-related health risks during renovation or demolition projects.

AHU (Air Handling Unit): A device used in HVAC systems to regulate and circulate air within a building or data center.

AIA (American Institute of Architects): An organization that sets industry standards for architecture and construction, including contract documents used in construction projects.

AMP (Ampere): A unit of electric current, often used in the context of electrical power distribution in data centers.

APM (Assistant Project Manager): A role that assists the project manager in planning, coordinating, and overseeing projects.

ARC (Attack-Resistant Construction): A design approach used in building data centers and other critical infrastructure to enhance the facility's resistance to physical threats, such as forced entry, blasts, or other forms of attack. ARC methods include reinforced walls, secure access points, and other structural enhancements aimed at protecting the facility and its operations from external threats.

ATS (Automatic Transfer Switch): A device that automatically transfers power to a backup source when the primary source fails, ensuring continuous power in data centers.

AV (Audio-Visual): Refers to the electronic media devices used for video and sound within data centers or other facilities.

Bacnet (Building Automation and Control Network): A data communication protocol used in building automation and control systems, including HVAC and lighting.

Bacnet Over IP: An extension of Bacnet that uses the Internet Protocol for communication, allowing for more extensive integration and control.

BAS (Building Automation System): A centralized system that controls and monitors the building's mechanical and electrical equipment, such as HVAC, lighting, power systems, fire systems, and security systems. BAS aims to improve occupant comfort, reduce energy consumption, and manage building operations efficiently. In data centers, BAS plays a crucial role in optimizing environmental conditions and ensuring systems are functioning within desired parameters.

BGP (Border Gateway Protocol): A protocol used to exchange routing information across the internet, critical for data center networking and internet connectivity.

BIM (Building Information Modeling): A 3D model-based process that provides architecture, engineering, and construction professionals with insights and tools to efficiently plan, design, construct, and manage buildings and infrastructure.

BIMCO (Building Information Modeling Coordination): The process of coordinating various disciplines within the BIM model to ensure design and construction efficiency.

BMS (Building Management System): Integrated software and hardware system used to manage a building's mechanical and electrical equipment, including HVAC, lighting, power systems, fire systems, and security.

BOM (Bill of Materials): A detailed list of all materials, components, equipment, and assemblies required to complete a project or a product. In construction and data center projects, the BOM includes quantities, specifications, and descriptions of each item, serving as a crucial reference for procurement, inventory management, and project planning.

BOQ (Bill of Quantities): A document used in tendering in the construction industry in which materials, parts, and labor are itemized.

CA (Contract Administrator): A professional responsible for managing and overseeing the execution of contracts in construction projects.

CAC (Cold Aisle Containment): A cooling strategy used in data centers where cold air aisles are enclosed to prevent the mixing of cold supply air and hot exhaust air from servers. This setup improves cooling efficiency by directing cool air to the front of the server racks, enhancing the overall performance of the HVAC system and reducing energy consumption.

CCTV (Closed-Circuit Television): Security cameras used for monitoring and surveillance within and around data centers.

CFR (Code of Federal Regulations): A codification of the general and permanent rules published by the Federal Government departments and agencies.

Change Order (CO): A formal document issued during a construction project that modifies the original contract terms, scope of work, schedule, or costs. Change orders can arise from unforeseen site conditions, client requests for alterations, design changes, or adjustments needed to correct errors or omissions in the initial plans. Each change order typically details the nature of the change, the justification, the cost impact, and any changes to the project timeline. Proper management and documentation of change orders are crucial to maintaining project control and ensuring that all parties agree to the modifications.

CIBSE (Chartered Institution of Building Services Engineers): A professional association in the UK that provides guidance and standards for building services engineering.

CM (Construction Manager): A professional responsible for overseeing construction projects, managing resources, timelines, and quality control.

CMS (Construction Management Software): Software used to manage construction projects, including planning, scheduling, budgeting, and resource management.

CO (Certificate of Occupancy): A document certifying that a building complies with applicable building codes and is suitable for occupancy.

COI (Certificate of Insurance): A document that provides proof of insurance coverage, listing the insurance company's details, coverage types, and policy limits. It's commonly required for contractors and vendors to ensure adequate liability protection during a project.

Colo (Colocation): A data center service where businesses can rent space for servers and other computing hardware.

CPM (Critical Path Method): A step-by-step project management technique for process planning that defines critical and non-critical tasks.

CT (Current Transformer): A device used to measure alternating current by producing a reduced current proportional to the current in the circuit.

DAS (Distributed Antenna System): A network of antennas designed to extend cellular coverage within buildings, often used in data centers to improve communication.

DCD (Data Center Design): Refers to the planning and layout of a data center, including considerations for space, power, cooling, security, and network infrastructure.

DDC (Direct Digital Control): A control system typically used for HVAC, lighting, and other building management applications.

D-Mark (Demarcation Point): The point where the responsibility of the service provider ends and the responsibility of the customer begins, often referring to the physical boundary between a public and private network.

DNS (Domain Name System): A hierarchical and decentralized naming system for computers, services, or other resources connected to the internet or a private network.

EIA (Environmental Impact Assessment): A process used to evaluate the environmental effects of a project, including potential impacts on the natural environment and human health.

EPO (Emergency Power Off): A safety feature that allows for the immediate shutdown of all power in a facility, commonly used in data centers for emergency situations.

ESG (Environmental, Social, and Governance): Criteria used to measure the sustainability and societal impact of a business or investment.

FABRIC (Flexible Advanced Binding and Routing in Computing): In data centers, FABRIC refers to a network architecture that provides a flexible, scalable, and highly available way of interconnecting multiple data center resources, such as servers, storage, and networking devices. The term is often used to describe a mesh-like network topology that improves data flow and resource utilization across the infrastructure. It enhances the management, automation, and performance of large-scale data environments, making it particularly suited for hyperscale and mission-critical applications.

FCU (Fan Coil Unit): A device consisting of a fan and a heating or cooling coil, used for individual room temperature control.

FAT (Factory Acceptance Testing): Testing performed at the vendor's facility to verify that equipment meets the required specifications before being shipped to the project site.

FTP (File Transfer Protocol): A standard network protocol used to transfer files from one host to another over a TCP-based network, such as the internet.

HAC (Hot Aisle Containment): A data center cooling strategy that encloses hot aisles to capture and contain the hot exhaust air from server racks. This approach prevents the hot air from mixing with the cold supply air, allowing for more efficient cooling and temperature control within the data center. By directing the hot air back to the cooling units, HAC helps improve the overall energy efficiency and effectiveness of the data center's cooling systems.

HVAC (Heating, Ventilation, and Air Conditioning): Systems used to regulate the environmental conditions in data centers and other buildings.

HVDC (High Voltage Direct Current): A method of transmitting electricity over long distances, used in some large data center applications for efficiency.

IBEX (Infrastructure Business Exchange): A platform for managing business processes, assets, and infrastructure, often used in data centers for operational efficiency.

IBMS (Integrated Building Management System): Combines various building management systems (BMS) to provide a unified interface for managing the overall building environment.

IDF (Intermediate Distribution Frame): A distribution frame within a data center that interconnects and manages telecommunications cables between end-user devices and the main distribution frame.

IPMI (Intelligent Platform Management Interface): A set of computer interface specifications for an autonomous computer subsystem that provides management and monitoring capabilities.

ISO/IEC 27001: An international standard for managing information security management systems (ISMS), critical for data center operations.

JIT (Just-In-Time): An inventory strategy used to increase efficiency and decrease waste by receiving goods only as needed.

KPI (Key Performance Indicator): A measurable value that demonstrates how effectively a company is achieving key business objectives, often used in project management.

LDS (Low-Voltage Distribution System): A system responsible for distributing electrical power at low voltage levels (typically under 600 volts) throughout a building or facility. In data centers, the LDS manages the distribution of power to various equipment, such as servers, networking devices, and other IT infrastructure, ensuring reliable and efficient operation. It includes components like switchboards, distribution panels, circuit breakers, and wiring, and is designed to maintain power quality and safety standards while accommodating the specific load requirements of the data center.

LEED (Leadership in Energy and Environmental Design): A green building certification program that recognizes best-in-class building strategies and practices.

LMS (Lighting Management System): A system that allows for the control and management of lighting within a data center or other facility.

Lon (Local Operating Network): A network communication protocol used for building automation, integrating various systems like HVAC, lighting, and security.

LT (Lead Time): The amount of time that elapses between the initiation and completion of a process, such as ordering and receiving equipment.

MDF (Main Distribution Frame): A primary hub for telecommunications wiring, distributing signals and connectivity to various parts of the data center or building.

MDP (Main Distribution Panel): A key electrical panel in a building or data center that distributes electrical power from the incoming utility service to various sub-panels and circuits throughout the facility. The MDP houses breakers, fuses, and other protective devices to manage and safeguard the distribution of power to different parts of the facility.

MOP (Method of Procedure): A detailed, step-by-step guide used during construction, maintenance, or other critical operations to ensure tasks are completed safely and correctly.

MSA (Master Service Agreement): A contract that outlines the terms and conditions between parties over an extended period, commonly used in vendor relationships within data centers.

MSDS (Material Safety Data Sheet): A document that provides detailed information on the properties, handling, storage, and emergency procedures related to hazardous chemicals and materials used in a facility. It includes information on potential health effects, safe usage guidelines, personal protective equipment (PPE) requirements, spill and leak procedures, and first aid measures. In construction and data centers, MSDSs are essential for ensuring the safety of personnel who may be exposed to hazardous substances, enabling proper compliance with occupational health and safety regulations. The MSDS helps workers understand how to handle materials safely and what to do in case of an emergency involving those materials.

MTBF (Mean Time Between Failures): A measure of reliability, indicating the average time between failures of a system or component.

MTTR (Mean Time to Repair): A measure of the maintainability of repairable items, indicating the average time required to repair a failed component.

NDA (Non-Disclosure Agreement): A legally binding contract establishing a confidential relationship between parties to protect sensitive information.

NOC (Network Operations Center): A centralized location where IT technicians monitor, manage, and maintain client networks and data center infrastructure.

OAC (Owner-Architect-Contractor) Meeting: A regularly scheduled meeting that involves the project owner, architect, and contractor. These meetings are crucial for maintaining alignment among all key stakeholders on the progress of a construction project. They serve as a platform to discuss project updates, address potential issues, review upcoming milestones, and ensure that everyone is on the same page regarding the project's goals and timelines. The meetings help in facilitating clear communication, resolving conflicts, and making timely decisions to keep the project on track.

OBEX (Open Building Exchange): A flexible data model and protocol designed for managing data exchange in building management systems.

OFC (Optical Fiber Cable): A type of cable that contains one or more optical fibers used to transmit light signals, which are converted into data. These cables are critical for high-speed data transmission in telecommunications, internet connectivity, and within data centers. Optical fiber cables are known for their high bandwidth capacity, low signal loss over long distances, and immunity to electromagnetic interference, making them ideal for supporting the fast and reliable data connections required in modern digital infrastructure, including hyperscale data centers and other mission-critical environments.

PDU (Power Distribution Unit): A device used in data centers to control and distribute electrical power to racks of servers and other equipment.

PMP (Project Management Professional): A certification recognized globally, demonstrating competence in leading and directing project teams.

PM (Project Manager): The professional responsible for planning, executing, and closing projects, ensuring that goals are met on time and within budget.

POP (Point of Presence): A physical location that houses servers, routers, and other network equipment, providing connectivity to the internet or another network.

QA/QC (Quality Assurance/Quality Control): Processes and procedures used in construction and manufacturing to ensure that products meet defined quality standards.

RACI Matrix: A responsibility assignment chart that clarifies roles and responsibilities in a project by categorizing tasks into Responsible, Accountable, Consulted, and Informed.

RF (Radio Frequency): Electromagnetic frequencies used for communication, ranging from 3 kHz to 300 GHz. In data centers, excessive RF exposure can cause equipment interference and pose health risks, requiring proper shielding and safety measures.

RFI (Request for Information): A standard business process used to collect written information about the capabilities of various suppliers.

RFQ (Request for Quote): A process in which a company solicits quotes from suppliers to purchase specific goods or services.

RFS (Ready for Service): In data center and construction terminology, RFS indicates that a system, equipment, or facility has completed all necessary testing, inspections, and installations and is now fully operational and ready to be used or put into service. This term is often used to mark the completion of specific project milestones or phases, indicating that the infrastructure is ready for customer use or further stages of deployment.

RPP (Remote Power Panel): A distribution unit that provides power to multiple racks or rows of servers within a data center, allowing for efficient power management and scalability.

RTU (Roof Top Unit): A type of HVAC unit installed on the roof of buildings, often used in data centers for environmental control.

SCADA (Supervisory Control and Data Acquisition): A control system architecture comprising computers, networked data communications, and graphical user interfaces for high-level process supervisory management.

SDN (Software-Defined Networking): An approach to networking that uses software-based controllers or application programming interfaces (APIs) to communicate with underlying hardware infrastructure and direct traffic on a network.

SLAs (Service Level Agreements): Contracts that outline the expected level of service between a provider and a customer, detailing specific performance metrics and guarantees.

Smart Hands: A service provided in data centers that includes on-site technical assistance for tasks that can be performed by technicians under remote guidance or predefined instructions. These tasks may include hardware installation, cable management, equipment maintenance, troubleshooting, and other operational support functions that don't require specialized knowledge of the customer's systems. Smart Hands services help reduce downtime and ensure that equipment is properly handled, making them a valuable resource for managing remote IT infrastructure efficiently.

SME (Subject Matter Expert): An individual with extensive knowledge or skills in a particular area, often consulted for advice on specialized projects.

SOC (System and Organization Controls): A suite of reports from an audit that covers information systems, particularly security, availability, processing integrity, confidentiality, or privacy.

SOV (Schedule of Values): A detailed statement provided by a contractor, listing the value of each work item in the project, used to measure progress and approve payments.

SPM (Senior Project Manager): A professional who oversees large and complex projects, providing leadership and direction to ensure successful project completion.

TCO (Temporary Certificate of Occupancy): A temporary certificate issued by local authorities that allows a building or part of a building to be occupied before the full completion of all construction work, provided that the space meets minimum safety and operational standards. It is often used in construction projects to enable partial occupancy while remaining work continues. The TCO is valid for a limited period, during which time the remaining construction or adjustments must be completed to qualify for a permanent Certificate of Occupancy (CO).

TCO (Total Cost of Ownership): A financial estimate intended to help buyers and owners determine the direct and indirect costs of a product or system.

TOC (Top of Cable): The point where the cable terminates at a device, often referring to the highest point in a rack or cabinet.

UPS (Uninterruptible Power Supply): A device that provides battery backup when the electrical power fails or drops to an unacceptable voltage level.

VAV (Variable Air Volume): An HVAC system that varies the airflow at a constant temperature, used in data centers for energy-efficient temperature control.

VRLA (Valve-Regulated Lead-Acid): A type of rechargeable battery commonly used for providing uninterruptible power supply (UPS) in data centers.

VOIP (Voice Over Internet Protocol): A technology that allows voice communications and multimedia sessions over Internet Protocol (IP) networks, including the internet.

About the Publisher

Justin DeFillippo is an author and self-publisher with a passion for sharing his extensive knowledge and experience in the mission-critical and construction industries. With a hands-on approach and a focus on practical insights, Justin aims to make complex subjects accessible to all readers.

For inquiries or to connect, you can reach Justin at defillippoj@gmail.com or visit his LinkedIn profile at linkedin.com/in/justindefillippo.

Justin is currently based in Flower Mound, Texas, where he continues to contribute to the field through his writing and professional endeavors.

Read more at https://www.linkedin.com/in/justindefillippo/.

www.ingramcontent.com/pod-product-compliance
Lightning Source LLC
LaVergne TN
LVHW090358210926
848480LV00002B/387